THE NEW

THE PROFESSIONAL PERFECTIONIST'S GUIDE TO GREATER EMOTIONAL INTELLIGENCE, A MORE FULFILLING CAREER, AND A BETTER LIFE

EMILY GOLDEN, PCC

ISBN: 978-1-7355601-0-6 (hard cover)
      978-1-7355601-1-3 (soft cover)

Edited by: Monika Dziamka and Amy Ashby

Published by Warren Publishing
Charlotte, NC
www.warrenpublishing.net
Printed in the United States

For my mother, Ellyn Mantell, my biggest advocate.
I would not be the woman I am today without you.
I love you more than you know.

TABLE OF CONTENTS

ACKNOWLEDGMENTS

This book would not be possible without the support of so many important people in my life. I am not able to name them all here, but they know who they are!

To my beloved Jeremy: your unending support, devotion and stability allows me to soar to new heights. Thank you for honoring all of me, for allowing me to be fully realized. Thank you for partnering with me to raise our two incredible children Maddie and Max, and of course, our fur babies DJ and Koty. With you by my side, everything is possible. I love you more every day.

To Maddie and Max: a mother's love is unlike any other. You are my heart and soul. I have learned more from raising you than I ever thought possible. Keep shining brightly. The world is yours for the taking.

To Mom and Dad: thank you for not giving up on me. I know the early years were tough. Thank you for modeling *joie de vivre* and a work ethic like no other.

To my sister Alli: We don't get to pick our siblings, but if I had a choice, I'd choose you. You are my best friend and my favorite person to laugh (and cry) with.

To my in-laws Meryl and Seymour Golden: thank you for welcoming me in to your family like your own almost twenty years ago. Thank you for modeling generosity and love always. Most of all, thank you for raising the father of my children, one of the kindest and most caring humans on this planet.

To Laura Schaefer: thank you from the bottom of my heart. This book wouldn't exist without you. You are brilliant, intuitive, and insanely gifted.

To my friends and extended family: thank you for enriching my life, for making me smile, for being there through thick and thin.

To my dear clients: thank you from the bottom of my heart for allowing me to partner with you on your journey, whether for a few months or many years. I learn and grow with you as much as you learn and grow with me.

And to you, my reader: I am grateful for the time and energy you have invested in this book. Honor your Golden Self. Treat yourself kindly. Know that anything is possible.

INTRODUCTION

*If we all did the things we are really capable of doing,
we would literally astound ourselves.*[1]

-THOMAS A. EDISON

*W*hat is *possible?*

Read that again, slowly this time. *What. Is. Possible?* For you? For your family? For your career? For your children?

I can't answer that question for you, but I have answered it myself over and over. And I can support you in your search for the answer—because I've been where you are: overwhelmed, stuck, struggling, confused.

Perhaps everyone in your life thinks you are super successful, yet you feel called to do something more, or something completely different. Perhaps you've created an amazing business or a high-level career, but you hesitate to take your hands off the wheel for even one minute. Do you put a lot of pressure on yourself? You've benchmarked yourself and your success based on the external world. This approach has been satisfying for short periods of time. But it's no longer working.

Maybe you're in a rut. The tricky thing about a rut is that you often don't know you're in one until you begin to come out of it. But there are signs:

- You move through life inches at a time, on autopilot. Going to work, coming home from work. Same routine, different day.
- You feel uninspired despite "having it all" on paper.
- You believe your mediocre career or life is as good as it gets.
- You find yourself saying some form of "it could be worse."
- You think, *I'll handle my discontent when things slow down.*

If you are thinking, *Who is this person, and why is she calling me out?* Let me put all of my cards on the table for you.

I have a spinal deformity that is pretty significant, as well as an invisible medical condition called Ehlers-Danlos syndrome (EDS). As a child and teen, I struggled with learning differences. My mom almost died when I was fifteen. She ended up needing twenty-two abdominal surgeries before losing her large intestine and four and a half feet of her small intestine. My Generalized Anxiety Disorder (GAD) is also part of the package. I happen to have a brain that's predisposed to anxiety. My guess is you and I share that trait. There are times in my life when I've been in a rut and times when I've been stuck in struggle and doubt.

And yet, big life challenges *ultimately have not stood in my way.*

I've created a beautiful family and a thriving business helping thousands of individuals like yourself. I like to think of myself as unstoppable ... not to boast, but to create a clearing for someone else.

I am *unstoppable.* And with a set of steps I'm about to share with you in the chapters ahead, some important mindset tweaks, and a paradigm-shifting New Golden Rule for life, you will be unstoppable too.

What is possible for you and for your life is bigger, better, grander, more staggering than you've ever imagined.

I'd like to invite you to discover it with me.

Your Golden Partner

I'm the friend to whom you can tell anything. You can trust that I'm not going to judge you. I'll disarm you so completely that you won't feel as if you need to hold anything back—even if you happen to be Type A. Even if you happen to be a high achiever. *Especially* then.

If you've been absolutely killing it, yet you're asking yourself, *What's next?*—you're my kind of person.

Are you a perfectionist? A *professional* perfectionist? It's as if, for you, the bar is always being raised. You're only as good as your last accomplishment. And as you accomplish more, the stakes get even higher. A perfectionist believes they can control—or that they want to control—the experiences other people have of them.

And that's just a lie. You can't. Both of my kids have Tourette Syndrome despite there being no history of Tourette's in the family. They are a constant reminder that no matter how much we try to control things, life has its own plans. If you've been getting similar reminders, you can be assured *I get it.*

You may be experiencing a feeling of never being fully satisfied with the life you have today. But before we delve deeper, let's pause a moment. I want to be super clear. What I will *not* be saying in the pages of this book is that the answer is to surrender and not strive for excellence. That would *never* work for me, and it wouldn't work for you, either. Instead, it's about learning to find balance between having high expectations and driving toward excellence ... and having room for your own humanity and imperfections.

Here is what you'll find in the pages that follow:
- A look at how perfectionism and over-productivity show up in my own life and in the lives of my high-achieving clients;
- The New Golden Rule and how to apply it to shift everything in your life, from your relationship with your spouse to your ability to ask for a raise at work or build a successful business;

- A three-step process for total life improvement that begins with an Archaeological Dig: identifying and separating your survival instinct and all its harmful tendencies from your Golden Self and its incredible gifts;
- Guidance on how to create your own unique vision for a more fulfilling career and life;
- Roadmap exercises to help you with the "how" of navigating life and career transitions or obstacles;
- Tips on how to overcome common Dig Dangers: the roadblocks and setbacks that often crop up for those who choose to push past old paradigms and Survival Self habits;
- A close examination of the four most important components of Emotional Intelligence (EQ) at work: Self-Awareness, Emotional Expression, Interpersonal Relationships, and Stress Tolerance;
- Coaching on how to build well-being, confidence, and optimism in order to make this whole process easier and more actionable.

Sound good?

Let's get started.

What's Possible?

In the pages that follow, I'll talk about the process of becoming that leader as well as the steps I've refined to help my clients get there faster and with greater ease than I did. The funny thing is, I'm the last person in the world who would ever write a book—primarily because I struggled with reading comprehension and spent so much of my childhood overcoming it. In fact, when I began to study coaching, my mother, who's a force of nature herself, said, "You're going to write a book." I wanted to tell her, "Stop putting your dreams on me!" I even said out loud, "If *you* want to write a book, *you* go write a book." I got quite resistant to the whole idea. I was on the phone with her, walking my dog DJ, when she said this, and I actually got *angry*. I felt my body flood with heat despite the near-freezing temperature outside. I unzipped my jacket and paused, arriving at the realization that this familiar reaction was a sign. There was something inside me that needed a closer look.

So, here we are. I wrote a book. (You were right, Mom!)

Why did I overcome my resistance and my fear and dive into this project—this book *that will not be perfect*? Because I could no longer keep all that I've learned to myself. I want you to hear my story and know this: *you can make your life more satisfying*. You can make your life more fulfilling.

From one perfectionist to another: it's possible.

There is no shortage of circumstances with which I deal. I am an example of the possible, of what it looks like to not give up.

And I want you to know that you can have anything you want. I want you to feel it in your bones. Because this world doesn't need more quitters or more victims or more perfectionists. This world needs more survivors and warriors and people who fight back, create, build, and show up in a big way.

To do so, I've created the most powerful tool of my career. It's called The New Golden Rule, and if you let it, it will change everything.

STEP ONE

THE ARCHAEOLOGICAL DIG

*In Greek Mythology, the Golden Age came first. It was
a period of peace, harmony, stability, and prosperity.
Its noble citizens lived among the gods in a state
of abundance to an advanced old age.*

*After the end of this first and best age came the Silver Age,
the Bronze Age, and the Heroic Age. The fifth and current age
is the Iron Age. The goal of so many of my clients is to
reconnect to the people they were in their Golden Age—the
early stage of life before they lost themselves—and to bring
that piece of themselves into the picture today.*

Chapter 1

THE LIES YOU'VE BEEN BELIEVING

Rather than wandering around in problem-solving mode all day, thinking mainly of what you want to fix about yourself or your life, you can pause for a few moments throughout the day to marvel at what's not broken.

—KRISTIN NEFF[2]

The occasional slap of the windshield wipers was the only sound in the car. He gripped the wheel tightly, looking straight ahead. I sat in the passenger seat, wondering if he was more afraid than angry or more angry than afraid.

I was in the middle of a major inflection point in my life and had just announced, "I can't do this anymore."

I was done … but not with him. No, I had to leave my well-paying, full-time job. I was unable to keep up the balancing act of fulfilling the duties of a big—no, enormous—professional role, two kids with special needs, a small side business, a chronic medical condition, and all the other stuff that comes up in anyone's life. For me, the "other stuff" had recently consisted of the very painful end to a friendship I had treasured. Correction: it wasn't just a friendship. It was a full-on obsession with very few boundaries, and its implosion had me questioning everything ... who I was, how I behaved, and what I really wanted.

I had spent the last year in a rigorous and transformational coach training program, so I knew *exactly* what would happen if I didn't make a big change. I would self-destruct, and my marriage and kids would suffer the fall-out.

He finally spoke.

"We're going to have to cut back on our expenses significantly. Things will have to change. I'm scared; I'm not going to lie. But I just can't see you struggling like this anymore."

A rush of emotion came up through me as tears began to roll down my face.

A year before, a conversation like this would not have happened. Could not have happened. I did not have the tools or the vision a year prior but by then, I did. I finally knew what I wanted professionally. And I *chose* to believe that I could have it.

And that night, driving in the rain, my husband did too.

You know that moment when you're sitting in a plane on the runway, and the pilot finally releases the brakes? The jet fuel gets the chance to do its job, and within seconds, all 175,000 pounds of your 737 is hurtling forward, ready to take off? To break the bonds of gravity?

That.

That moment is what this book is about. I'm going to help you find it.

Where are you right now?

Where do you want to be?

What's possible from that place that seems impossible today?

I want to begin by getting real with you and sharing how perfectionism, over-productivity, and other lies show up in my life, *and* how a game-changing rule I invented helps me achieve mastery over them, instead of the other way around. However, I want to mention that these topics are not something I'm calling forth from my distant past. I didn't look at my perfectionism and over-productivity and solve them once and for all. It is ongoing, challenging work. But I've made a lot of progress, and I know you can too.

Before we get into the nuts and bolts of my teaching, it's important to acknowledge where you are right now. If you're reading this book, my guess is perfectionism is playing at least a small role in what may be holding you back—professionally or personally. Let's look at two recent examples from my client base to give you a sense of what I mean. The names I use throughout the book have been changed.

Troy procrastinates. That, he knows. What he does *not* know, however, is why he does it. What is revealed in our work together is that Troy's need for perfection in his work quickly turns a project he's excited about into a burden, creating resistance and pressure.

My client Veronica has been talking about creating a scalable solution to sell to clients. We have been working on breaking up her fear of not knowing how to do each of the steps required. She is someone who always did well in school. She remembers getting less than an A only two times in college and that was the first time in her educational history. Today, she's struggling with tackling something over which she won't have total mastery from start to finish.

My own drive or need to be perfect continues to be reflected to me through the imperfections of my own body. As I mentioned, I have EDS, a connective tissue disorder, and a very rare and pretty severe spinal deformity, which you can't see. You might notice my neck looks a little bit stiff. But the fact is, I'm missing six discs.

The first year of my life, my head lay on my shoulder. Doctors thought I had CP—cerebral palsy.

My parents were *freaked out*. My mom said, "I'm going to do everything I can to help her." My dad threw himself in to his work. My aunt recently described to me that during my first year of life, I looked very fragile. She said, "None of us wanted to hurt you. You looked so uncomfortable." I was also kind of an ugly duckling as a kid. One of my eyes was lower than the other. One ear was inside itself—I was not pretty until I grew into myself as a teen. That was when my struggle with perfectionism began to unfold. Perfectionism came from my fear of losing this new attractiveness.

Paralyzing Perfectionism

My flavor of perfectionism is trying to control the way other people think and feel about me so I can reassure myself. It's not just a matter of "not being judged." I want to be thought of positively, *very* positively, and this has held me back from being fully exposed and speaking my mind. I have strong points of view, and when I put them out there, some people will agree with me and some won't. The thought that people won't agree with me has been difficult to accept.

My need to manage and control other people's perceptions of me hit an all-time high when I was in my late thirties. That need for control was paralyzing me in relationships and in my career. My life was starting to get smaller and smaller. I had a falling out with a friend who had been a close confidante for thirteen years, and it was heartbreaking. I didn't want my heart to be hurt again, so I withdrew, thinking, *I'm not going to ever have a close friend again; I'm never going to let someone in that close*—as opposed to being able to recognize that sometimes relationships have good reasons for pausing or even ending. Some friendships last a lifetime, but some last just a season, and that's okay.

Navigating the grief at this time in my life gave me the opportunity to take a close look at my need to control what other people thought of me. It held a mirror up to my perfectionism, which came out in full force for me as early as college. I went to school and I declared a major in accounting because my parents told me to. I didn't want that path, but I craved their acceptance and esteem. I thought, *What do I know? They know better.*

I was an accounting major for two years. I struggled. I didn't like what I was learning. My grades weren't great, but it wasn't the grades that were the main problem. The issue was the significant disconnect I was feeling from my work. I looked with envy at my friends who were studying psychology, sociology, and communication.

My father saw some similarities between him and me in our approach to life, in our brains, and in our drive. His stance was, "Go for what I did. I have the success formula." He went for accounting, got his law degree, and then became a practicing tax attorney, which could not have been further from what *my* drives and motivations were, but his path worked for him and he thought it could work for me.

I find this type of story in many of my clients' backgrounds. We are the type of people who try so hard, who did what we were told to do for a very long time. It's not uncommon, therefore, for individuals like us to have a reckoning at some point—to come face to face with the fact that it's time to live our *own* truths, as opposed to living within the well-meaning confines of someone else's vision.

My father had a very strong view of what generated satisfaction for people, based on his own experience. I had an interest in animals and art, but he didn't, and what I wanted more than anything was his approval. So, I suppressed these interests. The funny thing is, when I look at myself now, I can see all of the similarities in our two personalities that had him wanting me to follow in his footsteps. And I've ultimately done just that—in my own way. I am a businesswoman; he is a businessman. Our minds think in very much the same way. We're both very driven.

We share the good stuff, and I absolutely honor him for his success and see his influence in my wins as well. Still, I had to figure out my own path and I was met with resistance when I tried to follow my own internal guidance system. For example, if I wanted to do art and not tennis as a teen, it wasn't a conversation I was willing to have. I decided that I would rather have Dad's acceptance at that young age than stand for what I really wanted.

As I became an adult, I pursued many of the interests that I cared about deeply ... but did so on the side. From a career perspective, I worked hard to convince my father to support my plan to switch out of the business school and into the arts and science school at my university. I said, "I will go into business." I wasn't going to take my social psychology degree and become a therapist because he always said, "You're a businesswoman, you're a businesswoman."

From Parent-Pleasing to People-Pleasing

I moved into the arts and science school but was still on the business track. When I graduated, I got a job, for a split second, in sales, and then I moved into corporate human resources, and that's where I grew my career. In this environment, my perfectionism played out in the form of people-pleasing. A therapist of mine observed that I had put one of my first bosses into the role of my father. I was desperately working for my first boss's approval. I always wanted to please the people I was working with and for, and it was a winning strategy for me in many ways. People loved to work with me because I would always go the extra mile. The problem was, however, that my motivation wasn't pure. A lot of that motivation was caused by me thinking, *They'll accept me, and then I can accept myself.*

Of course, as Marshall Goldsmith said in the title of his bestselling book, *What Got You Here Won't Get You There*, I hit a place in my career where my approach was no longer tenable. I was being groomed for bigger and bigger roles and spreading myself thinner and thinner. I finally got to a point where I was like, *I cannot give anymore.* At the same time, I noticed I was sitting around tables with people who had strong viewpoints and who weren't afraid to put those viewpoints out there.

Yet *I* was afraid—deeply afraid—and, therefore, constrained.

I was afraid of being wrong. I was afraid of being exposed. I was afraid of being rejected. I was afraid of being disliked.

University of Houston research professor and bestselling author Brené Brown is a courage, vulnerability, shame, and empathy expert. She says perfectionism is a twenty-ton shield. And she is exactly right. Perfectionism, she said during an October 2013 episode on the Oprah Winfrey Network, is a habit designed to protect you from feeling shame (its permanent partner in crime) and help you avoid criticism, blame, or ridicule.[3] It's also an incredible burden, and the thing is, you don't *need* that kind of protection.

You are stronger and more worthy than you think you are. There is no reason to hide. Perfectionism is keeping you from being seen, just as it kept me from being seen.

Perfectionism is not the same thing as having high standards. Instead, it is a fear of failure, of looking stupid, of making a mistake, of being judged, of being criticized and ridiculed—and then having to feel that shame. As Marie Forleo says in her book, *Everything is Figureoutable*, perfectionism is rooted in fear. Perfectionism is the fear of not being good enough. In an effort to protect oneself from being judged by others, the perfectionist harshly judges herself. [4]

I have *lots* of practice in judging myself harshly—and so do my coaching clients. You'll read many examples throughout this book.

I hit a plateau professionally and experienced the negative consequence of a habit—people-pleasing—that until then had served me quite well. I began feeling more and more confined.

There was a woman inside me who was screaming to get out and have her voice heard. She wanted, of course, to be able to spend her time and her life doing work that lit her up. Yet I had created this crippling perfectionism inside myself. Fortunately, I kept getting messages from the universe to give it up—many times in the form of my health issues. The most recent nudge was my daughter's diagnosis with the same connective tissue disorder I have.

What could be more perfect for someone who has grappled with perfectionism than to know, at a cellular level, *I am imperfect and so is my family*?

A few years after my daughter's diagnosis of Tourette's when she was five years old I got the sense of, *It's okay. It's all okay.*

I believe you get to choose how you live your life. You have a choice of being a victim of your circumstances or the creator of your life—separate from your circumstances. I am very happy to say this is the person I am today, a person who makes strong choices. After doing a lot of work on myself and on the way I think, I've become the leader of my own life.

Unapologetically.

 PERFECTIONISM MIND MANAGEMENT EXERCISES

1. **Ask for and accept *imperfect* support.** For example, I coached a client of mine to simply ask her husband to load the dishwasher and practice being okay with the fact that he did the chore differently than she would. And the dishes still got cleaned!
2. **Conquer perfectionism. Take action.**
3. **Fail forward. Expect to fail. Reward yourself for failing!** It's about progress over perfection—small steps. You can't see hair grow, so quit watching it. Go about your life. Check back on progress in six months and you'll see it. Repeat Marie Forleo's mantra, "Progress over perfection." This has helped me and my clients in immeasurable ways.

4. **Calendar whatever it is you want to complete.
   Set a time limit and don't go over that time.** In
   other words, use time to constrain what you are
   working on. Getting tasks done and off your plate,
   even if they aren't done perfectly, will generally
   give you a huge sense of relief. When we don't
   constrain ourselves and then get to work, things
   start to pile up and we become paralyzed by the
   enormity of everything. Here's an example: a
   client of mine, Maria, was applying for a job and
   was asked to do a case study for the interview.
   She became almost paralyzed from the fear of not
   doing it perfectly, and she started telling me that
   the case study was going to take fifteen hours
   to complete. She didn't have that kind of time. I
   asked her how long she wanted to work on it, and
   she said two hours. I said, "Done. This employer
   wants to see how you work and if you're a fit. Two
   hours of your time is enough to figure that out."

GOLDEN KEYS

- People pleasers and perfectionists behave the way they do in an attempt to control what other people think of them.
- This is so they can compensate for their own negative thoughts—especially shame—about themselves.
- Perfectionism is a context, a story we tell about the world around us, so I work with my clients in conversation and in other ways to shift that context. This can happen in minutes or it can take months.
- One powerful way to break up perfectionism is to have a conversation with a friend or someone you trust who is not a perfectionist and ask for that person's perspective on a situation. They can help you look at facts instead of your interpretation.

EQ CONNECTION: WHAT IS EQ?

Emotional intelligence, also called EQ, enables us to make our way in a complex world. You can think of EQ skills as street smarts or common sense. Those with low EQ tend to rub others the wrong way, while those with high EQ are seen as charismatic, attractive, and warm. While this topic could certainly be a book (or twenty!) of its own, my intention with these short EQ Connections sections is to weave in an introduction to this important topic. Building EQ is a backbone to the work I do with my clients. I believe in adding these skills to the equation of a whole person. EQ is very important; it comprises the foundational building blocks of the self we work to unearth and bolster along the Archaeological Dig process.

Steven J. Stein, PhD and Howard E. Book, MD, authors of *The EQ Edge,* define emotional intelligence as a set of emotional and social skills that establish how we perceive and express ourselves. We develop and maintain social relationships with EQ, and our skill level in this area influence how we respond to the challenges in our lives, as well as how we use the emotional information we receive from others—in both our professional contexts and in our personal relationships—in effective and meaningful ways.[5]

Throughout this book, we are going to be looking at the specific areas of emotional intelligence I feel are the most crucial. These are self-awareness, interpersonal relationships, emotional-expression, stress tolerance, and happiness.

In thinking about how to define emotional intelligence, I often ask my clients who they knew at the top of the class in high school or in middle school. This person was very gifted academically and likely had a high IQ. However, oftentimes that person's success in life has been stymied since that time or eludes them completely. When I say "success" here, I'm talking about general happiness and fulfillment. It might be because this person with a high IQ lacks EQ, which is very different but arguably more important.

EQ is different from personality traits as well. It can't be measured by personality assessments like the Myers-Briggs Type Indicator or the DiSC assessment. EQ is something that changes over time. Those with high EQ are able to easily connect with people, which pays high dividends at work and in life in general.

Chapter 2

THE NEW GOLDEN RULE

*If you change the way you look at things,
the things you look at change.*[6]

–WAYNE DYER

Y ou remember the golden rule, right? Of course you do. It's
baked in to our culture in a million different ways.

The "Old" Golden Rule:
Treat others as you would like to be treated.

This sounds noble on the surface, but let's dig in to the message
here. You are being motivated by what you'll get back from
someone else—and you are assuming you know what other people
want or need, based on your own perceptions or imaginings. It
implies that feelings of satisfaction and happiness *come from other
people*—the way they do or don't treat you.

What is the impact of this way of being and acting?

It's stifling. And, often, completely ineffective. So, let's flip the whole thing on its head. As you read, think of the famous Beatles line, "... the love you take is equal to the love you make."

The New Golden Rule:
Treat yourself the way you want others to treat you.

When it comes to living our best lives, we've traditionally had it all wrong. Acceptance and fulfillment are an *internal* game. Striving for more is an unwinnable proposition, leaving us running on empty, creating burnout and disengagement.

When you treat yourself the way you want others to treat you, you are living fully in your power. You are at peace. Naturally, you will treat others the same way, since your relationship with yourself informs your relationships with others. You are what you think you are. People will perceive you the way you perceive yourself. This leads to authentic compassion, trust, love, and kindness.

From my experience observing my clients, I see them become more authentic and more fully expressed when they step into the New Golden Rule framework. Their guard is down when they are their authentic selves. They are able to hear anything without becoming defensive. They are willing to take responsibility. Being fully expressed means they feel free to speak their truths, to say what they believe. They are not walking on eggshells. They are not being who they think they should be; rather, they are being who they *want* to be.

When you follow the traditional, or "old," golden rule, you are treating someone else the way you want to be treated; i.e., you are being kind to someone else by holding the door for them. Or, perhaps you are listening to someone with a problem. For example, a friend comes to you and you immediately want to make them feel better, process what's happened, and offer different viewpoints. The old golden rule says you do this because that's how you want to be treated. The issue is this: most people are not treating *themselves* with this degree of care. They are not holding their own hand, seeking out varied perspectives, or treating themselves with kindness.

What is possible when we can show ourselves this level of kindness?

We know how we want to treat ourselves. We can look to the old golden rule and learn from it. *I want to be listened to, understood, heard, seen, made to feel important and like I matter.*

Unfortunately, we are often not looking at it this way: this is how I want to be treated *and* I can ask for what I need. "Family member, here is what I need—space to vent, assurance that I'm being heard."

An Invitation Instead of An Assumption

When someone comes to you with a problem, you might try to solve it. If I'm facing a problem, for example, I want to unpack it and look at the different angles, whereas when my husband faces a problem, he just wants a solution. Our needs are clearly different, so the old golden rule isn't particularly helpful. When we each treat the other as we want to be treated, we are missing the mark.

With the New Golden Rule, you're inviting people to understand *their* own needs—and actually communicate them to you—so they can get what they want, as opposed to the two of you being in "automatic mode" or assumption mode: *I'm nice to that person, but they're not nice to me, so I'm going to get righteous.*

Again, the golden rule says, "Treat others the way you want to be treated." Yet it sets you up for disappointment; it's a trap. The Dalai Lama doesn't go around doing things so that other people treat him the same way he treats others. Instead, there's a purity to how the Dalai Lama holds himself. It's the same energy held by other spiritual leaders such as Mother Teresa.

The idea of "what's in it for me" is a set-up for disappointment. It encourages our survival instincts, and it breeds righteousness, as in: "I would *never* treat someone that way." Any time we expect something, we are ultimately handing off our power. Sometimes, I see within my clients a need that's not being met. And, unfortunately, they are looking outside themselves to meet it: *I have a need; I recognize I have a need. I'm going to go to my friend with my need.* It's a set-up for disappointment when you hand off the need to someone else *and* have an expectation attached to how it should be met.

Our families are often a main source of this kind of disappointment, but it can happen in the professional arena as well. Sometimes I will hear a client say something like, "My work should speak for itself." They have a need for more recognition in their careers, but they won't ask for it or advocate for themselves. You need to be your own champion. The old golden rule doesn't create space for that.

The New Golden Rule does.

If you've ever thought to yourself, *I don't want to be boastful,* ask yourself if, beneath that statement, you are feeling underappreciated. For example, my client Patrice is such a powerful woman. However, when it comes to asking for a raise, or for a different job, she feels stuck. At the core, she's *really* afraid of being seen as entitled. She often berates herself with thoughts such as, *Who do I think I am for wanting x or y?* Patrice is afraid of being left without a job due to speaking up about her needs. As a result of this line of thinking, she's constantly putting her needs on the back burner. Doing so causes her to feel resentment, anger, and frustration. Additionally, Patrice has expectations that people will follow through on what they say they're going to do. As a result, she is consistently disappointed. It's not a good look for her.

So, what's the solution? If you've ever felt like Patrice, the key is to identify your own needs and energy sources—the activities, people, thoughts, and habits that *give* you energy versus those that drain your energy. The old golden rule fosters an expectation. Unmet expectations foster disappointment, which has you putting up walls. This way of thinking and behaving has you disconnecting and holding back. It wastes your time and energy. It also abdicates your power: *I want you to treat me this way, and if you don't, I'm going to hold back, cut you out, or be disappointed.*

Any rule that has you handing your needs off to someone else is unhelpful.

Recently, a new client of mine applied the New Golden Rule with helpful results. Here is what she said about it: "I was thinking about my 'dad stuff' after our call, and I realized I've been waiting for *him* to give me mad props for doing entrepreneurship my way ... for being both my creative self and growing into a business self as well. When obviously, what I need is to give myself mad props and stop waiting for him. I need to treat *myself* the way I've been waiting for others to treat me. If I simply refuse to budge on the idea of, *I'm doing awesome, I'm right where I'm supposed to be, I am killing it,* he will come around. And if he doesn't, it won't matter."

Do you see the power of this shift?

Is the New Golden Rule Selfish?

You may be thinking the New Golden Rule is selfish. I disagree. Consider the last time you were extremely hungry. With very low blood sugar, it's difficult to even *think*, let alone prepare a meal for someone else or offer others support. Taking the time to nourish yourself spiritually, emotionally, mentally, and physically is essential if you want to show up for others.

Let's return to the example of Patrice. She had repeatedly gone to bat for her people to get increases in their pay. For years, she had expected that her boss would do the same for her. And as you might expect, she was consistently disappointed. Instead of having the conversation she needed to have, Patrice created drama in her own head that went something like this: "If I were *really* that valuable, I'd be compensated ...." Over time, she became resentful. She was even thinking, "Maybe I'm going to leave this company."

When we had our first conversation, I pointed to her habit of devaluing herself, and also that she had expectations and assumptions that were not true. She was making up stories about what was going on. So, we spent a lot of time getting clear on her assumptions and interpretations. Then we spent time getting clear on her needs, desires, and beliefs in herself. When we were able to clarify those things, she still said, "I'm going to be seen as selfish, self-absorbed, and entitled if I ask for what I want."

This way of thinking is victim thinking. I responded by saying that not asking for what she wanted was equally as selfish, self-absorbed, and entitled because she was disengaged and not operating in alignment with her higher level of commitment to the organization. Her commitment was to show up for her company fully-engaged, but she was not doing so because she felt under-valued. In other words, no one was winning with the status quo. Not Patrice, not her boss, not her organization.

Once she got clear on all of her accomplishments (as people often fail to acknowledge their accomplishments and the ground they've taken), Patrice started to feel more empowered. When we gained clarity on all of that, the conversation could become one that was not centered on survival or fear.

Instead, from a place of empowerment, ownership, and experience, people can give themselves what they need, acknowledging themselves and clearly seeing what their desires are. Then, they can ensure that their needs are met from strength and power, not from a story about being victimized.

All of this work didn't necessarily mean Patrice was going to get the big increase in pay or the promotion. The old golden rule often comes with an attachment to some particular result. Conversely, with the New Golden Rule, you are aware of your need, and can still be curious and creative about how to have that need met—even if it's then met in non-obvious ways.

In this particular case, however, Patrice *did* wind up getting a big raise. She also got this crazy bonus that no one at her workplace typically gets. As a result, she is now a better leader for her team than she ever was before. Everyone wins. Instead of assuming what others are thinking, she is now able to ask herself, "What do I need? What motivates my behavior?" and then ask the same of her team members.

By getting curious and connected with her team, she is learning their specific and personal needs. Before, Patrice assumed her team just wanted money; now she is discovering that some team members also desire recognition, challenge, a supportive environment, and more. The flip side of assumption is awareness. The New Golden Rule challenges you to be aware of your own needs and desires and to get curious about those of others as well.

Action from Wholeness

From a young age, I told myself a story about how I was selfish. I hated the way "selfish" felt. As a result, I would overcompensate. I would go over the top with how I treated people; I would go out of my way to take care of people, even when they didn't ask for it. At work, I didn't want to just be a top performer, I wanted to be a *top* top performer. I wanted my generosity and extra effort to be recognized, because then I could disprove the label I had given myself. *See*, I would think, *You're not selfish! Look at how selfless you are!*

The only person who lost out in this equation was me. This way of thinking had me feeling undervalued, trying to prove wrong a false belief about myself. Of course, I was never going to be able to do it.

The work I've done since then is to give myself what I need. Then, from a place of empowerment and peace, I *want* to do nice things for other people and make a difference for them from my highest self, an idea we will explore in greater detail in the next chapter. My actions flow not from an attachment to an idea that a person must receive them in a certain way, but from a place of wholeness. This realization feels both peaceful and invigorating.

My process for using the New Golden Rule:

1. Identify a need within yourself.
2. Acknowledge when this need is not met.
3. Catch yourself creating a dramatic story about what's wrong and what needs to be fixed.
4. Halt the story.
5. Figure out how to get that need met.
6. Move forward.

The perfectionist context has both myself and many of my clients thinking we've always got to be striving for more. Personally, it has me feeling ashamed. The amount of shame energy I have spent in my life around the idea that I'm selfish is ridiculous. It's such wasted energy. Again, perfectionism is about avoiding criticism and judgment from others. It's not about being perfect. Instead, it's flawed thinking, e.g.: *Once I get to that next level, I'll finally feel valuable; I'll finally enjoy those feelings of contentment.*

I still do this with my body, telling myself, *When I reach this magical point, this magical weight, I'll be good.*

A client of mine, Nadine, does this with her relationship to time. She is constantly at war with time. While she has shifted to some useful thoughts such as, "I get to choose how I spend my time," she often comes up short and feels burnt out and exhausted. It's okay to prioritize business—she's right to have these big dreams for herself and her business, but we are still working on shifting her narrative regarding her time. Nadine needs to ask herself, *Who am I committed to being? What are the actions I need to take every day to be in alignment with that goal?*

It's not for anyone else to decide who Nadine is in this world. It's for her to decide and to live into that definition. This requires dropping an attachment to reacting to every event in real time. (I call this "Squirrel! thinking," inspired both by the Pixar movie *Up,* as well as watching how my own dogs behave outside.) Nadine also needs quiet time to just relax and swim in the pool. The shift toward showing up for herself and getting her needs met allows her to actually make the impact she is committed to making in her business, community, and life.

That is the New Golden Rule in action.

The Lies You've Been Believing

Now that we have a new rule for living, let's apply it to perfectionism and its lie that you can control how someone else views you. The thought behind this lie is that if you act a certain way or perform at a certain high level, another person will definitely like you and respect you. Or, on the flip side, if you say a certain thing, that same person will reject you.

It is a lie to think we can control how someone else will perceive us.

Our society trains us with proclamations such as, "Be nice to that person. Don't hurt their feelings," as if we have the capability to hurt someone else's feelings and someone else has the capability to hurt our feelings. I have had countless clients who have come to me and said some version of, "So-and-so was so degrading to me" or "so hurtful to me." What I always point out is that the other person didn't degrade them or hurt them with their words; it was the *thought* my client had about what that person said or did that hurt them. Tearing down this first lie is fundamental to breaking up perfectionism.

It's a lie that someone else can hurt your feelings, and we've been fed this lie from generation to generation to generation. We need to start challenging this idea so we can begin to understand its impact. If we understand that some people are going to like us and some people are not going to like us, that some people will judge us positively and some negatively, we will see how it is wasted energy to try to control how everybody views us. There's freedom in that understanding.

The second lie many people buy into is the idea that when we look a certain way, we will feel a certain way. Think of advertisements: the happy, thin woman with the man by her side. The notion is, *"Once I look like her, I will finally feel the way I want to feel. I will be happy*. I listened to a live coaching call through The Life Coach School, and a woman was being coached around binge eating. She asked, "Is it possible I could have Oreos in my house and not want to eat them?" The answer is, of course, "yes."

But the coach said, "Just know you will then move on to something else that is making you uncomfortable." The human brain is predisposed to discomfort. So, knowing that, wouldn't we rather create the biggest life we can for ourselves rather than obsessing about binging or obsessing about food? Let's put that energy into writing a book. Or starting a business.

Some people have this fantasy that once they reach a certain weight, life will be fantastic. I know people who've lost a lot of weight, and they do feel great for a period. But that happiness wears away, and they are left with the same feeling of inadequacy that they then apply somewhere else. So, the bottom line is: we need to take these lies we've been believing and turn them on their heads.

I'll never forget when Christopher McAuliffe, MCC, the senior leader who ran the first coach training program I attended, asked me, "Emily, do you know *how* to become an excellent coach?" I responded, "How?" as if he was about to give me the secret that would accelerate my journey and set me apart.

He said, "Be a really shitty coach faster."

Our kids don't go from crawling to running, do they? They learn to crawl and then begin to waddle around, using their hands to help stay upright. Then, they start stumbling around hands-free, looking like tipsy sailors. They fall. Sometimes they get hurt. They skin their knees. They learn from these experiences, and the next time they get up to walk, they adjust. Then, eventually, they run.

THE NEW GOLDEN RULE EXERCISES

1. **When you notice that harsh critical voice of self-judgment, ask yourself what a kind and compassionate friend would say to you about the thing you're judging yourself for.** This will have you uncovering unmet needs and identifying the disempowering ways you are talking to yourself. Now channel even just 10 percent of your friend's kindness into how you're talking to yourself.
2. **Lean in to the discomfort when you forge new habits or learn new skills.** While you do so, practice compassion and self-forgiveness. Embrace your humanity.
3. **Measure yourself, not against an expert in the field, but against yourself yesterday, the day before, the month before.** Growth is obvious and motivating when you measure yourself today against a former version of you.

GOLDEN KEYS

Apply the New Golden Rule when:
- You notice the harsh critical voice of self-judgment is present. Ask yourself how you would want a kind friend to speak to you about this very thing. Start talking to yourself that way.
- You notice a need welling up inside of you. See if you can begin being honest about what your need is. Don't expect others to guess or just know what that need is.

EQ CONNECTION: CAN YOU IMPROVE EQ?

Before I became certified in the EQi 2.0 assessment, I had done a lot of research on emotional intelligence. One of the reasons I chose the tool I did is because Multi-Health Systems Inc. (MHS), the organization that administers the EQi, had done a significant amount of research and had a large amount of data that proved it is possible to increase your EQ.

They looked at certain jobs and asked, "What are the emotional intelligence areas that need to be high to be successful in these jobs?" They also looked at marriages and people's general success and satisfaction in life. The organization proved through their data—and they have continued to build on their database—that it *is* possible to grow emotional intelligence by taking on specific practices in different areas.

It has been proven that we can impact and grow our EQ. We can train ourselves in the EQ qualities we need to succeed. EQ levels out the playing field because it's something you can work on, even if you feel your IQ isn't as high as your competition. Conversely, you can have a high IQ, but if you have a low EQ, you won't necessarily be as successful.

Studies have shown that over time we've warmed up, as a culture, to the value of having and growing our emotional intelligence. Of course, there are some people—and it tends to be more men than women—who run from the idea. Any time they hear "emotion" these people think soft, they think airy-fairy, they think EQ is a crutch, or that emotions don't have a place in business. But more and more, people are warming to the idea that EQ really matters.

When someone has a high IQ, they're usually swimming in a pond—professionally—with other people who have higher than average IQs as well. And the thing that really differentiates those who become successful, especially successful leaders in organizations or communities, is the EQ piece. Don't ignore it. If you have a high IQ, the demand to grow your EQ is even greater.

Chapter 3

THE TWO PARTS OF SELF

*No person, no place, and no thing has any power
over us, for 'we' are the only thinkers in our mind.
When we create peace and harmony and
balance in our mind, we will find it in our lives.*[7]

–LOUISE HAY

*W*ho are you when you are at your best?

Most of us go on automatic pilot in our lives. We just want to: 1. make it to retirement in our careers; 2. finish raising our kids; and 3. survive until our next vacation. As a result, we miss what life is actually about, which is all the moments in between birth and death.

I see all these people who only wanted to retire, and the irony is that when they do, they have no f - - ing clue who they are. In the realm of "career," which is where I work, the concept of surviving versus thriving appears in terms of surviving the layoffs and getting the promotion and getting to the next level, and then realizing that you are not the one in charge or the one who is driving your career. You're just surviving it. And there is a big gap between just *making it* through the day-to-day and actually *enjoying* yourself, actually contributing something meaningful to others, to the world, to your community.

What does it look like to thrive?

The key is to stop focusing on all of the things that are outside of yourself. Because no matter what, you will always have circumstances. There will always be good news and bad news. There will always be times to move quickly and times to slow down. Your kids, your parents—all of that—will always be in flux. So, it's about changing the mindset and changing the way you are *doing* your current circumstances. The way you are thinking about them.

That is where the access to thriving comes in.

Many people say things like, "Oh, if I start my own business, then I'll feel happy. Then I will feel fulfilled." They'll say to me, "Emily, you've started this business, you've created this life. I could never do that." I reply, "You're right. You could never do that. Because you have a different life. And what thriving looks like for you is different than what it looks like for me."

You have to realize that thriving starts with what you are thinking and which Golden Rule you are in the habit of following.

The Two Yous

There are two parts to all of us. People call the first and highest self several different things: your essence, your authentic self, who you are and have always been. I like to call it your Golden Self.

Then, there's the second self: your survival instinct, your inner critic, who, over time, can overcome and squash your higher self. This is your Survival Self.

Most people quickly learn to operate from the Survival Self. Your Golden Self gets lost and covered with debris, and that's not good, because you need to know your Golden Self intimately to follow the New Golden Rule.

We are not always great communicators with the Golden Self part of us. We don't relate to that part until the light goes on. So, the first part of the process I engage in with clients is something I like to call the Archaeological Dig. Through this process, we dig past a lot of dirt, expectations, cultural conditioning, family expectations, fears, and other nuisances to unearth your Golden Self.

There are several exercises that can be used during this dig. Here's one of them: I have my clients go out into the world and ask ten people who know them (colleagues, friends, and family) some powerful questions:

- When I'm at my best, what is the experience of being around me like for others?
- Who am I in my relationships with others? What are some of my notable traits?
- In what areas of life can I grow and develop the most?
- What is my most stand-out quality or ability?

One of the things my clients find, after going through this experience, is their buckets are fuller than they have been in a long time. And when they are filled up and feeling good, they are able to be more generous and kind to others through words of acknowledgment. The way I position this exercise is that we are working to get at the *Being* of an individual.

This Being is who you are—and always would be—even if you were to do nothing.

I also have my clients think back to their childhood and ask, "What did childhood Emily love? What lit her up? What made her sad?"

Animals, particularly dogs, have always been a source of joy for me. I love every type of dog. There's a Being about a dog that connects to *my* Being. It's a feeling of love, a cuddle, a connection, a need to be touched. That's part of my essence. It has nothing to do with accomplishment, as I'm always in the moment with dogs, and just being in the moment is enough. I watch myself parent my kids and parent my dogs and the comparison is so powerful. With my dogs, I'm like, "This is it. Your life right now, that's what it's about." It's not about getting in to college, getting married, having kids. It's not future-focused; it's totally in the present. The comparison is powerful because with my dogs, I'm not attached to any particular outcome. (My dogs are not well-behaved, but I am not taking any credit or blame for that.)

I've also always loved being outside. I love nature. I love laughing and being with my friends. I like being witty—not silly or slapstick—but witty. I like shopping and being creative and being deeply connected to others through stimulating conversations. When I was a child, my mom always called me an old soul because the things that came out of my mouth were profound. I'm sure you can see how reflecting on these longstanding qualities within myself ultimately led to my current path as a coach.

What will thinking about *your* innate qualities reveal to you?

The Golden Self

Many people who find themselves stuck in some area of their lives have one thing in common: they don't know themselves very well. This lack of self-awareness is, in fact, quite common. Knowing ourselves is key to personal growth and success. Maybe it is a little uncomfortable to contemplate, but a truthful look inward can help us move past our own obstacles.

So, how do we continue the Archaeological Dig? It helps to spend time alone with yourself. No distractions of any kind. Go old school with a pen and paper. No phones, no kids. (Books are okay.) Put yourself in an environment where you can really reflect, with limited potential for "Squirrel! thinking." You don't need a lot of instruction from me on this—do what works for you.

Next, have an intimate conversation with yourself. Ask yourself the tough questions. Be thorough and stay with it. Here are some examples:

- What do I want?
- What does my heart deeply desire? How will I know I've gotten it?
- How do I want to be remembered?

Your Golden Self is bright. It glistens. It's the buried treasure, the nugget of gold previously hidden under layers of dirt. Think of it as your own personal—yet extraordinary—lost city now uncovered. It has been exquisitely preserved and is just as magnificent as anyone could have imagined. It's where the sun shines its rays through the clouds. That place is the *You* that you know yourself to be.

When I am coaching, I know my client and I are onto something when they come to me and they're very disconnected from themselves but willing to start digging. We begin to talk about their highest self. They might say something like, "I would *love* to be that way," or "I would love to be seen that way," or to "be *that* person." "That would be amazing," they invariably sigh.

My job is simply to reflect to them the truth: "You already are."

I had a client recently, Andrea, who had a breakthrough in our second session. She said she had disconnected from the part of herself that was able to receive compliments and hear all that is good and right with her. But through exercises with me, she was able to see that part of herself. She recognized that if she were able to operate from that place, in that fashion, as a salesperson, she would be able to generate so much more business. She was then willing to take risks, to be bolder, because she felt fuller inside.

I work with a lot of individuals, especially women, who disconnect from the part of themselves that is a leader. They got this message when they were growing up that they were bossy, and bossy is bad, so, they rejected that part of themselves. In our work together, I say, "Bring that baby out. We must cultivate that." Here they are, in a leadership position, and they're holding themselves back from being the leader they truly are because of some limiting belief from their childhood that they'll be seen as bossy. And, sure, they *may* be seen as bossy. Or even bitchy. But if we as women don't start to take that leadership ground, we're never going to do all the things we are capable of doing. And then everyone loses.

The Survival Self

I'll hear, "I wasn't pretty/smart/cool/popular" a lot, and I have so much empathy for that kind of statement because there were areas where *I* wasn't enough. I had learning differences. So, in some ways, I really *wasn't* enough. In other ways, I was "too much." I was too emotional. I was too loud. I was too bright. When I started working in the corporate world, I distinctly remember a woman who said to me, "You always seem so happy," and she said it in such a negative way. I responded, "I am. I choose it." While I took it partly as a compliment, I also felt her pain. I sensed a tinge of envy because I had that pep in my step. I don't have that pep all the time, but I choose to embrace it when it's there. I do get that it can be too much for some people. In certain situations, I learned to dim my own light so as not to make someone else feel bad or uncomfortable.

Whenever we dim or curtail ourselves because we think that's what others want (old golden rule alert), we do so because we're afraid we'll be judged or rejected. This habit comes right from the Survival Self and it's not serving us.

There are a number of different aspects to the Survival Self, and a big one is Scarcity Thinking. With my scarcity clients, there is never enough time and never enough money. They create that context, that story, of "never enough" with whatever they're up to: never enough sleep, never enough profit, never enough attention. You get the idea. Scarcity mindset holds people back in a major way.

On the flip side is the Abundance mentality. Most people can't go right from scarcity to abundance, but just shining the light on the scarcity mindset helps. Where you choose to put your focus is exactly where you will see expansion. Wherever you put your attention, you will see gain. I have the opportunity to rain abundance in my life, in my family. And so, I just rain abundance.

I believe there is more than enough for all of us. It's not a competition. When Scarcity Thinking is at play, we think there are only so many resources and we've got to *get ours*. There's enough for everyone, yet we try to control and manage things as if there will never be more. When my clients show up with time scarcity, there's almost always money scarcity as well—and scarcity of other resources.

What is scarce for you? Time? Health? Love? Would it be possible to change your story? Your own value or worth?

Survival Self Stories

Survival Selves are often about controlling and managing. For example, my desire to control how my daughter, now fifteen, "does" friendship is a sign of my own survival instincts trying to protect her from the pain I experienced in childhood friendships and relationships. (And to protect myself from having to see her discomfort.) Meanwhile, I'm mapping my own past friendship "stuff" onto her. And I'm completely dishonoring her experience, which looks very different than mine.

Another manifestation of the Survival Self is giving up on yourself. It starts with little quits, and eventually, you've given up completely on a goal you once said mattered to you a great deal. You might have committed to reduce your sugar intake, for example, but then you say something like, "Well, *today* I'm going to have something sweet." What happens is, over time, your Survival Self tells you that you can't be trusted, and then you perpetuate that idea by quitting and proving yourself right. You say you're going to get up and go to the gym. Then, one day, you don't. That's a little quit. Then, you start quitting on yourself constantly. I often work with my clients on building the muscles of integrity and of trust in self.

Have you ever said, "I'll get to me later?" It's all about your family, the people you work with, whatever. "I'll just take care of everyone else, and then I'll get the last licks." There's a little bit of martyrdom there, and often a lot of resentment. That is fully a Survival Self mindset, and it comes from following the old golden rule instead of the new one. The Survival Self says that if you take time for yourself, you're selfish. I hear this one *all* the time, and it is not helpful.

We each have a few Survival Selves. Drama is another Survival Self tool: "Can you *believe* what happened?" There are people who have a lot of common and challenging stuff going on in their lives, but to them, these things are so much bigger and so much worse than they are for other people. Indulging in dramatic storytelling and thinking is just a way that their Survival Self is holding them victim.

One of my own Survival Selves is super dramatic, and I know it. I can feel it when she's coming on. She wants to make everything bigger. She exaggerates. She almost lies! She's *not* lying, but it's close. This survival approach was created by me, for me, when I was a kid and I wanted to get my father's attention and approval. He was very busy building a business and I thought, *If I'm dramatic, he'll hear me.* I don't like that piece of me, but again, it's a Survival Self habit.

Finally, some people have a story that they have to be a hero. Some of my clients get distracted from what they're creating in their own lives because they are so busy saving other people. The last people they save are themselves. The political environment right now is ripe for the trained eye to notice other people's Survival Selves. I see a lot of people who are uber-victimized by today's political climate. Political upheaval and twenty-four-hour news are huge distractions for people.

Practice Seeing Your Survival Self

It is eye-opening to me how quickly some people get it, can see their Survival Self, and then separate themselves from their Survival Self stuff. Other clients will gain clarity, then an hour after our session, they're back in their stuff. Everyone has their own journey and their own gradient, so I have to pay attention to that in my work with them and not rush anyone. Including myself.

My own Survival Self still shows up in my fear of looking stupid. I so vividly remember fifth grade and being friends with the smartest kids in my class who were getting test scores in the 90s. I thought I knew what I was doing, but I kept getting poor grades. So, I made up stories about myself. That storytelling is what still gets in my way. I'm much more cognizant of it now, but it's still there.

I had a Survival Self attack recently, in fact. I took my new puppy to puppy kindergarten. She's in training, and we were in the room with all these other puppies and their owners. The instructor was giving instructions, and I noticed a familiar feeling of anxiety coming over me because she was moving fast and I was not quite following the instructions. I was lost. She gave the instructions again, quickly, and my Survival Self was screaming: *You don't know what you're doing! You'll never get this! This is so hard, and yet everyone else can figure it out.*

It was an awful feeling, yet a very, very familiar one. So, we started doing the exercise and I couldn't figure it out. I'm looking around the room. One of the teachers came over and asked, "Are you going to start?" I said, "I don't know what I'm doing." It hit me that this used to happen to me all the time when I was in school. I didn't understand my learning differences then, so at an early age, I built up all these stories about not being smart and not being able to do things in a "normal" way like others could. My differences always had me feeling as if I wanted to escape. I'd find myself thinking, *I just want to leave. I don't want to be here.*

That's how I was feeling that day at puppy kindergarten. But at this point, I've done so much work on myself that I was able to pull one of the instructors aside and say, "Look, this isn't working for my learning style. I think I'm going to need someone to come to the house and repeat and repeat and repeat before I can start to learn and model this."

I know I will learn, although I have to say, training this puppy has been difficult. There is a part of me that wonders, *What if I can't? What if this time I cannot succeed?* That's obviously not my Golden Self; that's my Survival Self.

On the way home, I called my mom to check in for the day. I told her how I had felt during the puppy training class. My daughter jumped in to defend me, saying, "They were moving too fast, and I can help you." It was super sweet. And my mom said, "Look how far you've come." I acknowledged all of this, but it was nonetheless interesting to me how those old feelings of inferiority still cropped up. I was more anxious than usual.

Survival Self at Work

I am working with a client named Jessica who is looking to make a career pivot. She was laid off from her previous job. Her Survival Self has her very scared that she's going to be found out in terms of having been let go, and that all of the missteps she feels she made in her prior job will be discovered. She feels she needs to hide them.

As she prepares for job interviews, she's spending time coming up with ways to hide or distract the interviewer from this secret she's holding. I call what she's doing the "dead body in the trunk."

Jessica is clearly coming from a place of fear in her job search. We know her Survival Self is in action because she's engaging in a fear-based conversation. And this behavior is absolutely impacting her job search; she's not showing up as her most empowered, authentic self since she feels like she has this big secret she needs to hide. So, in our time together, we have been focusing on honesty. We're working on telling her story from an empowered place, where she is truthful about what happened in the last job and she is able to speak to what she has learned and the professional development she's garnered from the experience. And, as she continues her job search, she has completely transformed. Jessica is so much more confident, and she doesn't feel as if she's hiding anything. She is able to speak to her past failures as areas in which to grow.

Here is another example: I am working with a small business owner named Matt whose Survival Self has him gripping the wheel very tightly to control and manage how the business operates. Of course, this makes sense to a degree. He is the person who started the business, and he wants it to operate at a certain level of excellence. But his Survival Self—and its need to control everything—is blocking his business from being able to grow to the next level because he's afraid of taking his hands off the wheel. That would require handing over some responsibilities to new team members, maybe hiring someone to do some of the work he's been doing.

Gay Hendricks, psychologist, teacher, and author *of The Big Leap*, refers to this kind of situation as someone's Upper Limit Problem.[8] It's a common thing that happens with leaders who get to a certain level of success. They recognize—like I did with the help of one of my own coaches—that, as Marshall Goldsmith reminds us with the title of his best-selling book, *What Got You Here Won't Get You There.*

And Matt, in order to grow his business, has had to lean in to the discomfort of bringing in additional resources for his organization, and asking for support. He can't do everything.

Matt is a CEO. We've worked on shifting his mindset toward being CEO rather than just being this guy who started his own business and figured out a way to do things successfully. He's got to be able to grow, learn, and then back off. Taking his hands off the wheel required trust—trust in others, and trust in himself. It required him to feel uncomfortable because he can't control everything now. He doesn't know how each detail will play out. In developing that ability to lean in to what's uncomfortable, he's seen the greatest growth. Matt's business has nearly doubled over the course of our work together.

I have another client, Jean-Luc, whose Survival Self has him making everyone else stupid, idiotic, wrong, or lesser in order for him to feel better about himself. While this has him coming across to other people as obnoxious or arrogant, it represents his own insecurities and his own fear at play. This habit of judging other people all stems from this fear, of course, that he's not enough. He has created this way of comparing himself to people mainly around intellect. It makes him feel elevated in the moment, but ultimately crappy about himself and who he is as a leader. We've been working on identifying the fear behind his behavior, and what his Survival Self does with that fear. His judgmental nature can be a repellent for other people. Others don't get to see his true greatness. His judgment of others blinds him and blinds them.

Clients who come to me and say, "I am not happy at my current company. I'm not happy in my current role," often need to face down their Survival Self to move forward. They're not fulfilled, yet their Survival Self has them *completely* convinced that there is no way they're going to find work elsewhere, for one reason or another. The story might be that they don't have experience at another type of company; they can't pivot to another type of role. They are fearful based on this thought: *What if this is as good as it gets? And I'm going to give this* up?

Scarcity comes up again. They start to believe that there is a very limited number of opportunities out there. Believing *this is the best it's going to get,* is a disempowered way to live, of course. This belief impacts the employee's engagement with his or her organization. It has the employee becoming resistant and frustrated. So, I work with the individual to look at true facts versus the story they are telling to make a shift. We really get clear about the fear and the reality that, in order to make a change, there is going to be discomfort, and that's okay. They can survive discomfort.

You can take a risk and see what else is out there. You can better enjoy the work you're doing now once you see that there is a choice. The Survival Self aspects I most frequently help my clients to work around include owning, accepting, loving, and embracing where they are now in their journey.

My final example of Survival Self at work involves a client named Jay who was *sure* he was going to feel a certain way when he got to a certain point in his career. He would feel the level of satisfaction he was looking for ... once he got a particularly significant title. I'm sure you can see where this is going. He got the title and nothing changed in terms of how he felt about himself and his life. It didn't solve all of his problems. *Money* didn't solve all of his problems.

That's a Survival Self conversation because he's looking for outside validation to be okay. And it never, ever works. Survival Self serves us when there is an actual predator at our backs. The rest of the time, it mostly creates problems.

How to Discover Your Golden Self

Whenever you're faced directly with yourself, you might retreat by playing on your phone, getting a snack, turning on the TV, playing music, getting sleepy, grabbing a drink, or finding another way to distract yourself. If this sounds familiar, you may be avoiding the opportunity to get to know yourself. Perhaps the idea of it is just too uncomfortable.

Try truly connecting deeply with someone for thirty minutes, and you're likely to gain insight into what that person is all about. You'll see their strengths and have insight into their weaknesses, and you'll get a picture of why their life may be less than ideal. Yet when it comes to yourself, you can't quite figure out why your career and/or life isn't going as well as you'd like it to.

You likely have a deeper understanding of someone you hardly know than you have of yourself. If your intuition is telling you this is true, or if the examples of Survival Self above sound familiar, use the following daily practice to uncover your Golden Self:

1. **Set aside time to be alone each day.** This can be ten minutes at the beginning or end of your day. The only requirement is that you be by yourself, completely alone, without distractions—no books, no phone, or anything else you find entertaining. It's just you and yourself. It's okay to feel a little bored; embrace it.

2. **Have a conversation with yourself.** Pretend you are a person you are trying to get to know:

   - *What do you do for a living? Do you like it? Really, you don't like it? Why do you keep doing it?*
   - *What's most important to you? Why? Has this changed over time? When?*
   - *What are you afraid of? Why?*
   - *What are your strengths and weaknesses?*
   - *What was your childhood like? What would you change about it if you could? Why?*

3. **Review your life from the very beginning.** Think about the painful experiences you suffered as far back as your childhood and how those shaped you. How did these experiences affect what you believe today about relationships, work, parenting, money, leisure, meaning? What would you tell yourself if you could go back in time?

4. **Next, think about what you want for the future.** What are the challenges in your life right now? What do you wish you were doing? Have a conversation with yourself about the things that make you cringe because you wish they were different. Stay with it. At some point, it's likely you'll say to yourself, *This is stupid. I'm wasting my time and have other things to do.* This feeling is just fear or shame, and

it doesn't mean anything. Let the thought go by. It's your brain's attempt to maintain the status quo and not look at the difficult stuff to make changes.

5. **Meditate.** In addition to having these conversations with yourself each day, learn how to meditate and make it a regular part of your life. Guided meditations from apps like Headspace are a great place to start. Avoid judging your thoughts. Just observe and accept them.

Few of us have taken the time to examine our lives or ourselves. Our culture trains us to look at others and notice their weaknesses— sometimes quite accurately—even if we barely know them. Yet, we often can't see the things that others can see in us immediately. We have a habit of distracting ourselves from the truth. I invite you to put an end to the struggle you've been experiencing in your life. Once you do, you'll pave the way for creating a life that's more meaningful and satisfying.

Honoring Your Newly-Unearthed Golden Self

Putting what they've unearthed above ground in a shrine of its own is an important part of the process I take clients through. I want my clients to take that Golden Self of theirs and put it in a glass case, so to speak—to showcase it and protect it.

The idea is to honor this piece of you and remember it exists. Bring it "above ground," own it, and share it with others as a fully expressed human. Using the Golden Self as a filter or *lens* to approach life, career, and leadership opportunities is the key. When a situation comes up, and one of my clients reacts in a way that doesn't seem to be serving her very well, I help her to get grounded in her Golden Self—meaning I remind her who she is. Then, we look at the situation again and ask, what is her commitment through the Golden Self lens? How do things look different from the perspective of her highest self? What is the next action in alignment with that commitment?

GOLDEN SELF EXERCISES

1. Expect your Survival Self to whisper or scream in your ear: *This is hard; You're never going to pull this off;* or *Who do you think you are?* Get playful with the noise: *Oh, Perfectionist Polly, I know you are trying to take the wheel to keep us safe like you did when we were ten years old. But I've got us this time!*

2. When you notice you're spinning, ask yourself, *What's the right next move?* Ask, *What would [insert name of a hero/role model] do?* This strategy is not meant to infer that your role model has the answers and you don't. Rather, it's meant to point you toward doing something different, anything different. Coming up with a different perspective and acting from there can be so helpful. If all else fails, take a break to exercise, have a dance party, do yoga, eat a healthy snack, play with the dog … anything to break the cycle of reaching and grasping for "the answer."

3. Practice patience. This is a muscle most of my clients need to build. Sometimes this means *taking a day off.* My coach once said to me, "Emily, unlike most people, you don't need more rigor and discipline to get work done. You need more rigor and discipline to hold yourself to *relaxing.*"

4. Practice proactive planning. You are going to run
    into problems and roadblocks. It's a case of not
    if but when. Decide ahead of time: who will I be
    when there is a setback? What will I do? Remind
    yourself that when the going gets tough, the
    tough get going.

 GOLDEN KEYS

- Perfectionism is one of many Survival Selves we
  turn to. Whenever a Survival Self shows up, I
  work with the client to recognize it and then ask,
  "Coming from your Golden Self, what's the next
  step?" "What shifts?" "What is there more of, and
  what is there less of?"
- Complete the Archaeological Dig to get to the
  true desires that are showing up in your life
  right now. When you think about attaining these
  desires, notice if fear comes up.
- Fear isn't something to be scared of. It's energy
  to look at and be motivated by.
- Excavate and fully embrace your highest Golden
  Self so you can follow the New Golden Rule from
  a place of wholeness and possibility.

EQ CONNECTION: EMOTIONAL SELF-AWARENESS

Emotional self-awareness is the first of five specific elements of emotional intelligence I'll discuss. I'm including these five because I think they are powerful competencies to develop for living the New Golden Rule.

Emotional self-awareness encompasses the whole purpose behind my work. This kind of self-awareness is defined by Steven J. Stein, PhD and Howard E. Book, MD, authors of *The EQ Edge*, as the ability to 1) *recognize* your feelings, 2) *differentiate* between them, 3) *know why* you are feeling these feelings, and finally 4) *recognize the impact* your feelings have on others around you.[9]

Developing emotional self-awareness is such a key part of stepping into our own power. Here is an example of what I'm talking about. One of my clients is a successful engineer-turned-VP. That sounds great, but unfortunately, he has capped his own success because he lacks emotional self-awareness. If you told him, for example, that he is an impatient person—and a lot of people *have* told him this over the years—he would act like it was the first time he had ever heard that. He doesn't see it. He would deny it, shrug it off. The heart of our work has been taking a critical look at his resistance to seeing himself the way others see him.

Another client's anxiety shows up in an intense need to control the environment around her. She is over-focused on the way things look, and she would prefer perfection. It comes out a lot with how meetings are run and beating deadlines, even when doing so isn't necessary and puts undue stress on other team members. The impact of this way of working is she's never able to be present in the moment. The energetic impact (for her direct reports) of being near all of this angst and anxiety is considerable—and very taxing.

If this person were able to acknowledge her feelings, call them out, and say something like, "That's my anxiety speaking," it would cut a lot of tension and create additional positive results in her business, ones she's not yet able to imagine.

The New Golden Rule leads us to take a good look at ourselves. It has us generating self-awareness: *What is it that we want? Who is it that we want to be?* The old golden rule stymies self-awareness because it keeps our focus on other people and on making assumptions.

A lack of emotional self-awareness is something that comes up a lot in my work, and it creates such wide-ranging problems for people—in all areas of their lives—that I will return to this concept throughout the book.

I recently had an angry CEO as a client. While she knew she was angry, she was also having a lot of turnover in her company. She didn't connect the two.

I work with another leader of an organization who is incredibly insecure. He makes up all these stories in his head about what's going on in any given situation, and the stories are often not correct. Even when they are accurate, he puts himself through so much unnecessary inner turmoil. As a result, he comes off as preoccupied and distant.

My Own EQ

The best example I have of diving in to this idea, however, is from my own life. When I was in my coach training program almost five years ago, I introduced myself in front of the room. We were doing an exercise, and I talked for five or seven minutes. When I stopped speaking, I was asked *who I would be without the struggle and the suffering.*

Whoa.

This was the first time that had been reflected to me, the first time I considered that my story contained more struggle than it needed to. I had considered myself to be a pretty emotionally self-aware person, but I encountered—in that moment and during my training—that I tended to have a need to create drama in my life. As I began to unpack this tendency in myself, I realized how this habit of mine had impacted the people around me.

A couple of weeks after that day, I became friendly with a woman I had been practicing yoga with. She made a comment that also opened my eyes. She said that when she first met me, the impression she had was that I was serious. I guess she didn't get the warm, friendly Emily; she got an intense, disconnected Emily.

These two experiences served as an opportunity to get outside myself, reflect on who I was being, and consider the impact of who I *am* being on the people around me.

Who are *you* being?

SELF-AWARENESS EXERCISES

1. Grab a piece of paper and a pen.
2. On your paper, write down all the judgments of other people that are swimming around in your head today. Let it all hang out. This piece of paper is yours and yours alone.
3. Now read what you've written and star all the judgments that you also have of yourself.
4. Think about this and remember, what we can't be for other people reflects what we can't be within ourselves.
5. Take a few deep breaths. Feel your body. Remember you are human. You are not perfect. Forgive yourself.
6. Now find compassion for the people you are judging. They, too, are only human.
7. Rinse and repeat daily.
8. Watch the world shift around you.

STEP TWO

LIVING THE NEW GOLDEN RULE

In Ovid's Metamorphoses, *the Golden Age is both a place and time. During this era, nature and reason were considered in harmony. This balance made it easy for people to live in peace with themselves, with others, and with the world.*

Chapter 4

CREATING THE VISION

If you're not in the arena getting your
ass kicked on occasion, I'm not interested
in or open to your feedback.[10]

–BRENÉ BROWN

You can have *everything* you want.

So, what do you want?

Once we know who you are—your Golden Self—we are able to clarify your life's dreams, desires, and wants so you can fully live the New Golden Rule. I'd like to be clear that I'm not talking about dreams of running for president. That might be someone's true vision, but I'm more interested in the littler dreams. For example, when I started going through this process myself, I became acutely aware that one of the things I wanted was space in my life to be quiet. That was actually a vision of mine—to get connected to my body. Stillness. So, this second step in the process of total life improvement doesn't have to be this lofty, "I will become X." Or, "I'm going to be on Broadway." It *can* be something like that but, oftentimes, when we can just connect to the truth inside of us, we find basic human needs that aren't being met.

The time I spend in quiet reflection mode, whether it's meditating or journaling, is key to navigating this part of the process myself. The first thing I had to do was quiet myself. I was blind to what I wanted. I was going off of what I was *supposed* to want, or what was supposed to satisfy me. My next step—once I understood who I was at my essence and broke through the noise of my Survival Self—was simply realizing, *Wait, there is something inside of me that needs space.* I had to quiet myself. It's an ongoing practice.

I did a lot of writing. There's something powerful for me in writing every day. I sit down each morning and do about ten minutes of free-writing. I will do this forever. I write about what I want.

The thing about building a vision is it's not a one-and-done task. Vision is like a tapestry. For me, it has filled itself in over time like a painting. It reminds me of Georges Seurat's *A Sunday Afternoon on the Island of La Grande Jatte*—a huge canvas done in pointillist technique. Paintings done this way look like nothing in the beginning, but over time, they start to take form. Eventually, you stand back and there is this incredible rendering of the scene in a park.

That's what has happened with my vision over the past four or five years.

Not only did I need the quiet to *create* my vision, I needed the quiet to *continue to manifest* my vision. My vision for my life is that there's ample time and room to do the things I want to do. I've done vision boards, but I don't do it in a prescriptive way. My vision board is a hand-drawn picture featuring dogs, yoga, nature, people. I'm connecting to people. It includes a lot of love. It includes being a light—a lantern—for other people's visions.

I work with humans who spend a lot of time on the analytical side of life. You've heard of humans, right? Those big-brained beings who spend so much time just lost in their own thoughts? So, when these humans and I step into a vision-focused conversation, it's outside of their comfort zone. It's not prescriptive. I can't tell them what the next step will look like. It feels almost unproductive or indulgent. And we just need to be open to those feelings. I tell them to prepare themselves.

1. Reflecting

I like to begin by taking a look at the experiences that have lit my clients up in the past. Peak experiences. These experiences are so personal, and may include things like having a baby, running a marathon, or getting in to a certain school. These could include milestones like climbing a mountain, or quieter things that give a person joy. These could be moments in their career, working on a certain project, shining in a meeting or presentation, etc. This is an opportunity for my clients to see the ground they've taken. To look back and say, "I did that. And it meant a lot to me."

Dogs have been a passion of mine ever since I can remember. I studied them as a kid. When my grandmother took me to the bookstore on Saturdays, I'd find a new dog book to get lost in. I turned to books because I did not have a dog of my own until age thirty-seven. While so much has changed about me throughout my life, my love for dogs has never waned. Dogs make me feel alive. Dogs make my heart swell.

- What was *your* childhood passion?
- How did it make you feel?
- What actions can you take in your adulthood to reconnect to that passion?

2. Values

Next, I look at values with my client, not from the Survival Self but from the Golden Self. Values are unique to each person; they include the things that are important to a person. Family, achievement, and connection are common, but my clients and I come up with ten to twenty values that are unique to the individual. It's not productive to believe we all have the same values.

For example, I deeply value my friendships, but spending time calm, alone, and with my family on the weekends is even more vital to me. So, sometimes plans have to shift to accommodate this value. Once we understand our own values, we can live our own humanity and make room for others to live theirs as well.

Here is a list of common values; see which four or five of these leap off the page for you:[11]

- Family
- Adventure
- Honesty
- Achievement
- Acknowledgment
- Equality
- Authenticity
- Fitness
- Freedom
- Friendship

- Excitement
- Fairness
- Fun
- Justice
- Industry
- Gratitude
- Independence
- Romance
- Pleasure
- Spirituality
- Love
- Order
- Power
- Respect
- Flexibility

Then, for each of the values that you've selected, write about 1) how you are currently expressing them in your life and career and 2) how you *want* them to be expressed in your life and career, both in the short and long term.

3. Mindset

During this part of the process, I look for the barriers or the blocks that are in my client's way. Where she is playing the victim, I call her out on *that*. Where he is taking responsibility, I call him out on *that*. I was trained in coaching *context* not *content; I look* for the filter or the story an individual is living though. This is one reason you cannot rely on your close friends to coach you—they often use the very same filters you do to parse the world.

An example of a filter at work is a thought my client Patrice shared with me during our work together: "I am taken advantage of and I don't know how to play the political game here at this organization. Therefore, I miss out on the opportunities that I deserve."

When I hear this, I'm not interested in looking at *who* did *what*. Instead, in this particular instance, we actually took a look at where else this filter showed up in her life—where Patrice was missing certain cues and was not getting what she believed was her due in terms of salary. In other words, this was not a story that started today or last month. It started in her childhood when she realized that her parents were simple folks who didn't know "the system."

Her parents had never gone to college and didn't know how to educate her the right way, or the way she believed was the right way. She always felt behind because of what she had missed growing up.

When we get to the root of a certain filter or belief, we can shift it to better serve ourselves where we are now in life and in our careers.

Here is another example of unpacking a mindset. Jeanne frequently tells a story of having an insatiable child inside of her. As a kid, she always felt like she was getting last licks, or missing something she needed. Jeanne was one of five children, and by the time the food got to her at the table, there was not enough left. For her, this mindset of insatiability most obviously shows up around food, but it also shows up around being recognized at work. She feels that no amount of recognition would ever be enough. So, I said, "Okay, let's take a look. What's the age of this conversation?" She said, after a long pause, "I was five years old when I remember feeling this way for the first time." Digging in to the question did wonders for her.

For Jeanne, just making this connection was enough. We didn't have to spend a lot of time on this to root it out and shift the story. She ultimately was able to handle urges and temptation around food more intentionally.

4. Visioning

Next, I ask, "What is it we are trying to create here?" It could be a career pivot, career growth, or a shift in other areas of life. Sometimes

I work on building overall well-being or better relationships with my clients. We will identify a gap, for example, in the person's ability to pull in resources or take risks in relationships. In my process, we have to understand where we are going.

You would never go on vacation without having a destination, right? So, when you engage a coach, she is going to want to identify the goal. I ask, "What is the meaning of what we are talking about?"

I'd like to talk for a moment here about the power of choice and belief when it comes to planning for your life, or helping your children flourish. Here's what I mean. A couple years ago, my kids spent seven weeks at sleepaway camp. When they were each diagnosed with Tourette Syndrome at age five, I didn't believe this would ever be possible. Yet they both grew beautifully during their time away from home and had a great experience despite some typical homesickness and social challenges.

Medications were managed seamlessly, and both of my kids felt "normal" as their bunkmates frequented the infirmary for their own meds. So many kids take something on a regular basis, which certainly helps to normalize the experience for kids like mine.

I spent the time while the kids were away reflecting on the experience of them being at camp. What I noticed was a mix of anxiety (*What if they aren't happy? What if their tics flare and they are made fun of? What if they don't get enough sleep and they become overly emotional as a result? What if ... What if ... What if ...?*), excitement that we could all handle the separation, and the awareness that part of the reason the kids were able to go away was simply that my husband and I *believed they could*. We had confidence that they would be okay.

Who we are in our parenting—supportive, doubting, trusting, nervous, all of it—is absorbed by our children. When a child has special needs, the natural worries of raising a child become amplified. I understand that on a cellular level, given my own experience. Yet what I didn't know until I began the journey into my own inner work is that even a parent of children with differences gets to choose. We get a say in how we relate to them, how we relate to ourselves as their parent, and how we relate to their unique journey.

- I choose to relate to my children as whole and perfect just the way they are.
- I choose to stand for them, to push past discomfort and overcome obstacles with pride.
- I choose to notice when my own fears about who they are (and who they are not) creep in to the space so that I don't map those fears onto them.
- I choose to honor and embrace their differences.
- I choose to learn from them and to love them fully.
- I choose forgiveness for myself and for them in the moments when I forget all of this.

If any of this resonates with you, I invite you to get intentional about who you will be as a parent and as a leader. Make this choice boldly, then post reminders in places around your home where you look often: the bathroom mirror, the back of your front door, in your bedroom. Practice self-forgiveness when you forget your choice (because inevitability you will), and then get back on track.

5. The Coaching

Two of the best ways I can serve my client are 1) as an accountability partner, and 2) as an idea generator. I check in with them on practices from the last session. Where do they see traction? Where are they stuck?

Sometimes, we create new practices. Again, I am an accountability partner, but I ensure I am not the only one. This means it is important my clients have other sources of accountability, whether it's a friend, family member, a checklist, or a journal to track progress or new actions.

I empower my clients to leverage other support structures in their lives. I want to see them move forward, not create a codependent relationship. I refuse to become the person they resist and make excuses to run from when they have "failed" at a practice, or the person they need to "impress" when they think they have done it all.

One of the things that makes me highly unique as a coach is what I did professionally before becoming a coach. I was a corporate Director of Talent Acquisition and have seventeen years of experience under my belt developing talent and recruiting leaders. As a result, I offer my clients all the tools of my coach training, and I'm also able to serve as their expert consultant in all areas of career growth. I've worked with so many hiring managers; I've been a part of hundreds of interviews. What does that mean? It means at times, I take off my hat as a "coach" and give specific advice and expert guidance for their professional goals.

That experience makes me uniquely able to see someone's talent, even when they don't see it themselves. I am able to see what they offer, what they bring to the table, their skillset, so they can position those assets in the best possible way in their career.

One of the reasons I left talent acquisition is I was tired of looking at what was wrong with candidates when I was so drawn to what was right with them. I saw potential and hidden talents, but my job required me to focus more on deficits and blind spots. In any case, the best part of serving as a consultant to my clients today is that I get to draw out their hidden gifts and help them cultivate those positive attributes. I can help clients look at where there are strengths and where there are gaps.

Along the way, having a managed mind—meaning the individual has taken the time to get in touch with their Golden Self and identify Survival Self tendencies—is very important if you want to move in to a specific position eventually. Get in the door, acquire the needed skills, and move to the place you want to be in your career and in your life.

How I Navigated This Creation Step

Four years ago, I was working full-time for a $2.5 billion chemical company. I was carrying a full load of responsibility, working forty-five to fifty-hour weeks, maybe even more sometimes, and I had a team of people to lead. At the same time, I was in a coach training program that was every third weekend of the month for a year. It was a rigorous program that included a weekly coaching session, which was invaluable while I was learning the coaching basics.

The way that anyone learns best, in my experience, is hands-on. So, we were pushed out of the nest early, from the first weekend, to start taking on clients. I am so glad I didn't know the extent, the amount of time, that this program would demand of me. I was just so excited to jump in. I didn't have a clear idea of, *I'm going to do this, and then I'm going to leave my corporate job.* It was more the sense of, *I need to grow myself; I need to do something different. I think coaching is a thing I could eventually grow into.*

Coaching was a dream. I knew I needed to start moving toward the dream because I had been clear for many years prior that I wasn't doing what I wanted to be doing for the rest of my life.

So, I enrolled in the program. Before long, I was working with clients at night and on the weekends. My kids were ten and seven years old at the time and my husband was working full-time. It was a lot of juggling. The good thing was, I worked my day job from my home office, so I didn't have to budget time for a commute. That definitely helped because I could see clients before and after work.

Then, I got promoted at work to a director position. Of course, my team got bigger and my level of responsibility grew. But I used the opportunity to pitch to my employer the idea of having me do some leadership coaching for them. I started working with just one person. My employer was not on board initially but they trusted me so they gave me a chance. The coaching expanded to a second person because I saw the opportunity. Then, my employer came to me and wanted me to coach a third person. I worked with two emerging leaders and one established leader. These were high-potential individuals who the organization was looking to develop. So, that was awesome.

When I graduated from the coach training program in July of 2016, I was feeling very stretched. My kids had gone to camp and I had time to finally reflect and say, "This is what I want for myself. I want to be able to do this work full-time." Of course, that was a very scary conversation to be having. It was scary for my husband. He was super supportive, and I was working a lot. But I knew I couldn't continue at that pace. I thought, *If I can just continue to work full-time at my corporate job for another year, we'll have enough money in the bank so I can pivot.* I set a goal for myself: I wanted to have an extra $20,000 in the bank to give myself a few months to build my business.

What was interesting was that when I got that promotion, my salary increased *almost exactly that amount.* My bonus also increased. I wound up with the money in the bank before I expected it to be there. I also was starting to see more and more interest from others in my coaching.

Still, I was scared to make the leap. So I worked with my own coach, who I continued to work with long after graduation. With my husband's support, I was ready to make the leap sooner than originally planned. Part of the reason I had wanted to act when I did was that I wasn't feeling well. My health had started to decline because of all the work I was doing, and my age, and the reality of my degenerative condition. I thought, *If I don't do this now, if I don't build a business* now *with freedom and flexibility, I run the risk of completely burning out.* With my own business, I knew that when I did have flare ups, I'd more easily be able to take breaks. I just loved the idea of being able to turn off if I needed to.

I recognized that if I was going to buy in to my fear-focused brain and all the fearful thoughts around my plan to build and run my own business, there was no way I was going to be able to enroll my husband in that path. So, I had to do my own work to separate myself from the fear stories my own mind was telling me and just believe in what was possible. When I brought my plan to my husband, I had so much compassion for his fearful reaction, I didn't get defensive, or angry, or hurt. I didn't have all the responses I probably would've had if I'd tried to do it a year earlier. That's the power of coaching. I had done so much work on myself that I realized, *Oh, right. His reaction is* his. *It's his own fear.* After many conversations, he came back to me and said, "I believe in you."

Financially, it was a stretch, but we could swing it. And we did. I'm proud of who I was being in that moment of my life. I didn't get caught in the fear of it. I just kept my eye on the prize.

Part of that prize is that I continue to get more and more selective about the people I want to work with. In addition to being able to take on the amount of work that suits my health and life best, I am working with the type of high-performing individuals I feel best benefit from my expertise. At the time of writing this book, I'm on track to far exceed my corporate salary this year, yet that was not at all a motivator for this transition in my career. This was not expected, *and* it's wonderful.

EXERCISES FOR CREATING YOUR VISION

1. Get connected to your Golden Self by thinking about or journaling about what life will be like in all of its different areas (family, work, community, leisure, home) coming from your Golden Self 99 percent of the time vs. your Survival Self.

2. Write about two to three peak experiences you've had. How did these experiences make you feel? What did they reveal about your Golden Self?

3. Take a deep breath, close your eyes, and use your imagination to conjure up a version of yourself ten to fifteen years in the future. Where does this Future Self live? What are you wearing? What are your favorite things to do? What are your values and interests? What is a typical day like?[12]

4. Get artistic. Draw your vision, or create another artistic rendering that prompts you to remember your invented future.

5. Record yourself speaking your vision and listen to it over and over.

6. Go for a walk and notice what catches your attention or where your mind goes when you allow it to wander. What does this tell you about what you are naturally drawn to and what you want more of in your days?[13]

7. Collect old magazines and cut out pictures or words that represent what you want for your life one, five, or ten years from now.[14]

8. Make a list of people you admire. These can be individuals you know personally or people you're exposed to through the media. What about their lives or their work would you like to incorporate in your own life or career?

 GOLDEN KEYS

- Consider this: being a parent is being a leader. As parents, we lead the way for our children: we train them, we guide them, we advise them, we give them "feedback" to improve and be the best version of themselves. We challenge them, we point to their strengths and support them to develop in those areas. We give the very best of ourselves in service of our children's growth—and this is one of the reasons I *love* coaching parents to be better leaders in their careers. We often don't have to look too far to identify innate leadership skills and gain clarity on what's possible.
- Jumping right in to action from the same mindset you've always had causes only incremental shifts at best and often leaves you right back where you started. Action from insight—this is what causes transformational, lasting shifts.
- You can try to sell me on a limiting story about yourself and what you're capable of. I will just refuse to buy it.

EQ CONNECTION: INTERPERSONAL RELATIONSHIPS

The second emotional intelligence element I want to cover is Interpersonal Relationships, the ability to establish and maintain mutually satisfying relationships based on both give and take, in which trust and compassion are expressed in words and behavior by both people openly. This element is probably my biggest area of strength as an individual and as a coach. It's my edge. Interpersonal relationships are absolutely critical to me, and I believe they are absolutely critical to success in life.

There was a Harvard study a few years ago that looked at marriages and found that the happiest men, on their deathbeds, were the ones who'd had strong marriages. They were happiest throughout their lives. People who have strong relationships have richer and fuller lives.

When I say emotional intelligence is my edge, what I mean is I've innately known how to connect with people for my entire life. I learned very young from my mom who modeled this ability; the focus on the other person is engrained. When someone is in front of me, for example, I automatically get curious about them. I notice something about that person and comment on it. It could be something he is wearing or a look on her face, an energy I'm picking up. Or, I may talk about a current event or the weather. I'm always truly curious about the other person, asking questions. Of course, because I'm a coach, these skills have been refined and honed. I was good at it before, but now I'm much more masterful at it. I'm always looking for a way to connect to the person next to me or on the phone.

This was a habit I cultivated—proudly—in the corporate setting. I wasn't necessarily the smartest, the best trained, or in ownership of the most impressive degrees. But we know that most of the time in high-performing environments, we've generally got people with above-average IQs. So, the only differentiator is EQ. While I have a higher than average IQ (I know this thanks to evaluations in my primary school days), many of the people I was working with had higher IQs than mine.

However, in many cases their interpersonal relationship skills weren't as strong. How I learned to operate at an early age and then in my corporate life was to find a common theme between myself and others. I would often allow myself to be vulnerable, and share something going on with me. When my kids were young, I might've said, "I'm trying to balance everything, and I have to find childcare tomorrow. One of my kids is sick." I wouldn't complain, but I would share with the intention of creating some kind of personal connection. I cannot overstate how important this kind of communication is in a business environment.

We are people. We are humans. We are not like Flat Stanley, one dimensional. We have work problems that become personal problems and personal problems that become work problems. I always try to find the common thread. Once a person starts opening up and talking about herself, she might say something like, "Oh my gosh, I have kids too, and it's so much work trying to balance it all." I would say, "How do you do it?" I'd get curious and ask a lot of open-ended questions. Or, the person might say, "I don't have kids, but I have a niece and nephew," or, "My kids are grown, and I remember those days; they were so challenging." So then, I'll ask questions about that.

Fast forward to three weeks or three months later. I've created an association in my mind that Jan has three kids. When I see her, I immediately say, "Hi, Jan, how are you? How are your kids doing?" People feel connected when they're seen. It builds trust when someone remembers details about them. Now, I'm not saying that everyone has this skill; we're all skilled in different areas. I can't remember a damn thing I learned in social studies or economics, but I can remember that Jan has three kids and that she appreciates it when I ask about them.

One way to get better at interpersonal relationships is to make a mental note about these details. I may even say to myself, *Remember the first initial of Jan's son's name. His name is Jason and they both have 'J' names*. I'm going to store that fact away. Create intention for such an action. People can feel when you are truly interested in them. When they feel that, a defense gets released. They feel safer, and are therefore more likely to trust you and reveal themselves. They then have a desire to work with you.

Another awesome way to build relationships is through storytelling. For whatever reason, when I say, "Do you want to hear a story about that?" Or, "I have a story," people are into it. There's something soothing about those words. It must remind people of childhood, of curling up with a parent or a grandparent. So, I share stories. This is not anything that I *strategized*. It's just what I now know I naturally do. I was reminded of this gift when I started working with Rich, my coach.

We can look around us, in our communities, in the news, and see the brilliant mind who struggles with interpersonal relationships. And then you see the smart person who you just know has this knack for connecting with other people. It's that person who has you feeling important when you're in conversation with them. I would much rather have a person who I'm in conversation with walk away feeling like *he* is important, rather than me walking away feeling like *I'm* important.

When people come to me for coaching in business, I get curious about their relationships outside of the workplace as well as inside the workplace. We can see such clear patterns in how the individual engages in relationships. If we're going to go deeper, there's always a mirror in terms of the relationship that one has with one's self.

Give and Take in Relationships

A lot of women I work with are the main caretakers in their relationships. I don't mean this in the sense that they are in charge of the care of one person. I mean that generally, in life, they have this caretaker mentality, where they're constantly giving. Giving, giving, giving. Eventually, a depletion happens. I have been guilty of this myself. I've actually flip-flopped between being a giver and being a taker. Neither—being all one way—is healthy. Now, I'm very clear about boundaries and it's something I have to work on all the time.

Caretakers tend to have a lower self-regard, so it's almost as if they're buying the relationship, or feeling like they have to overcompensate in order to feel worthy to be in the relationship. You'll notice this by their constant need to do nice things for people. I notice this in certain relationships I have had, and what's fascinating to me about this is that the people who are constant givers say they don't expect anything in return, but they still become resentful when they don't actually get some sort of recognition for all they do. At first, it seems sweet, but after a while, it almost feels uncomfortable, disingenuous. I have a very strong antenna for over-functioning and over-giving, being in the line of work I'm in. The gap I see is there isn't enough time spent on the caretaker's own unmet needs because they may never express them.

The caretaker has a very hard time receiving and feels very uncomfortable when someone is wanting to help them. This can cause breakdowns in creating real intimacy in relationships. We all, as humans, need support at different times. We want to be the ones who give support and we want to be able to receive support. It's important that we are open to be supported. Many of my female clients—and some men—don't even know *how* to receive support. Women often get the message, probably from their mothers and grandmothers, that they're the ones who are supposed to take care of people and that asking for support is a sign of weakness. So, how can we build that muscle of asking others for help? A lot of times with clients, I will set up a specific action or a few actions for them to take, where they are intentionally asking for support. I send them out into the world to do some interviews, and that's the first step in asking for someone's support during the coaching process.

On the flip side is the taker. That's the person who is constantly asking for something or who is constantly expecting the other person to show up in a more available way. I like to look at these relationships as sixty/forty or seventy/thirty. They expect the other person to give sixty or seventy percent. Generally, takers are looked at as arrogant or self-centered. I've swung the pendulum this way myself. As you work on fixing caretaking tendencies, it's important to keep an eye on balance.

Positive Expectations

What I noticed in my work with clients, and in my own life, is that when we have an expectation of other people—that they're going to show up in a certain way, or that they're going to respond in a certain way—and those people don't meet this expectation, we become disappointed. Having realistic expectations is the key, rather than making meaning, or creating a story, when someone doesn't respond to you the way you think they should.

For example, let's say you have an expectation that someone will call you with a certain frequency, say each week. If they don't call one week and you make it mean that they don't care about you, they don't love you, they're not a good friend, you'll become hurt by it. This kind of thing shows up in personal and professional life often and is detrimental to interpersonal relationships. On the flip side is having a realistic conversation in your head, something like, *Everyone has their own interpretation, or idea, about how frequently to call. Everyone has their own interpretation about how much information to give.*

I see this often in business, where one person is not super communicative. They're working on something, but they're not telling the other person involved what's going on every step of the way. The other person worries that they're not working on the project. So, the bottom line is that expectations in relationships can be dangerous. I'm not saying we should be in relationships that aren't fulfilling or satisfying. But we also have to recognize when our own expectations are getting in the way of us being able to connect with someone.

If you're working with someone who is much more introspective, introverted, or analytical and they don't communicate every step of the way, don't assume that they're not working at all or contributing equally. You can lay your expectations out at the beginning of your work together: "Hey, here's the type of communication that I do well with. What works for you?" Take ownership and responsibility.

Chapter 5

FROM BROKEN TO WHOLE: COACHING TOOLS FOR FOLLOWING THE NEW GOLDEN RULE

There has never been and never will be another you.
You have a purpose—a very special gift
that only you can bring to the world.

–MARIE FORLEO[15]

What is the story you tell about yourself?

To live fully from the New Golden Rule, it is essential to take a close look at the story you hold about yourself. Is it serving you? Is it an empowering story? Mine was not, for a very long time. Let me explain.

Until about five years ago, I related to myself as broken and needing to be fixed. I wouldn't have told you at age thirty-eight that I related to myself that way, because I didn't see it. Through deep coaching and self-awareness work, I learned I was constantly looking outside of myself for the answers. I was constantly looking for the thing that was going to make me feel better about *me*. (This was obviously before I had invented the New Golden Rule.)

As a kid who had learning disabilities, it was anything but predictable that I would ultimately end up on the A-track by eighth grade. I had a very long journey to get there; I was schlepped from doctor to doctor to try to figure out what was going on. Above-average IQ, challenges in school, what's going on?

My dad did not want me flagged and labeled at school. He thought this would be the worst thing for me. My mom was my fierce advocate, seeing to it that I got the support I needed. My parents were both amazingly supportive. However, there was still a lot of fear about what was going on with me and what I would become.

It wasn't the sense of, *I'm broken, so I'm giving up.* It was more like, *I'm broken, I'm going to figure out how to fix myself, and Mom and Dad are going to help me.* As a result of this idea, I was always striving. I would take on this challenge at work. I would jump into that new project. I would go the extra mile. I was always looking for something to fix myself.

I've talked about the fact that I have a spinal deformity. My images are frightening to both the trained and untrained eye. You can know nothing about anatomy, and you would still wince if you looked at my spine on a CT scan. I've seen onscreen models of my body that you could twist 360 degrees with a mouse, and in the images there were ribs coming off at weird places, missing discs, all of it. But I could always cover that up. My thought was that if I could just have my *exterior* look a certain way, then no one would know about what was really going on with me. Like, I could be okay; it would be okay if everything *looked* okay—whatever "it" means.

There is definitely reassurance from our culture when you're an attractive girl and then become an attractive woman. I leaned a little bit too much on that. I know that I didn't always speak my truth because I was feeling, *Well, I'd rather be accepted and feel good.* But for me, ultimately, it always went back to, *I'm broken. And I don't want anyone to know.*

So, my story as a young adult was, *I'm internally broken because of my spinal stuff.* I'd also had the learning differences. And then, in my late teens, an anxiety disorder that had been brewing got worse.

Tough Transitions

During my first year of college, my anxiety was so debilitating that I became depressed. It was frightening. This happened one other time in my life; such situations were connected to transitions. A lot of people struggle with big transitional periods in life. To this day, I have so much empathy for people navigating through such times because I've been there.

When I'm transitioning, I don't know where I stand. And when I don't know where I stand or what people think of me or how accepted I am, I go into that "fight, flight, or freeze" place.

It was my first semester of freshman year, and I was so depressed. My sister was at the same school and she called our mom, saying, "I don't know what to do with her. I'm so worried about her." The message I was hearing again was, *You have this disorder; you are broken, but we'll get you fixed up.*

Many of the therapists I saw over the years were reassuring. They wanted to make me feel better. What I actually thrive with, however, is the thing many high achievers need: a clear reflection of who I am and an honest reflection of who I'm not. I was really struggling, barely getting a 2.5 GPA, but I ultimately ended up getting multiple 4.0s by the time I graduated. This happened in my corporate career as well. I started off feeling apologetic for making a very measly salary and ended up walking away feeling like I was worth every penny. It is the theme of my life: face resistance, then create triumphs, over and over again. When I am committed to something, *I don't stop.* I get there. And I get there all in.

I believe this work is so powerful because it's all about this idea: *You are whole and complete. You are not broken. You are not damaged. There is nothing wrong with you.*

From that place of wholeness, *who do you want to be and what do you want to create?*

We don't have to be victims to our circumstances. We can fulfill our own needs. This idea was the most powerful thing I learned during my year of coach training.

In that mix, I learned how to create and present a package of perfection for others. I remember a friend telling me that another woman had asked her, "What does Emily's house look like? It must be perfectly decorated. It must be perfectly kept." (It's not, by the way.) But that *is* how my grandma's house was. I love my grandma, but I couldn't live with that level of perfection, especially because I love dogs and animals so much. Things are going to get messy. Nevertheless, hearing that woman's idea of me, of my home, was really telling. You don't see yourself until someone reflects it. I'm not perfect, but there's something about me that keeps coming off that way.

As a coach to my clients, I am constantly reflecting what I'm seeing and where there are gaps between someone's reality and the package they are trying to present to others. I make assertions about a client's blind spots. Sometimes I miss the mark, and other times, I'm exactly right. I tend to know I'm spot on when a person gets a little bit defensive about whatever it is I am saying. Usually, they'll come back around and remark, "You said this thing three weeks ago, and I've been thinking about it."

Letting My Inner Coach Shine ... Finally!

Anyone, anyone, anyone can go get coach training. But there are certain people who head in to the training who are already coaches. Those people have been coaches and leaders in their lives already. So, coaching is just a term that we use now for something that was simply called leadership previously.

I have been a coach since childhood. My earliest memories are in middle school when I just *led*. Maybe it was that I had struggled early on academically, and I had been in therapy, and so I had a level of self-awareness that some of the other kids didn't. I don't know if that's what it was. I don't know if it was my spirit, but I just always had it. Girls would come to me, boys would come to me, and they would share things with me that they wouldn't share with anyone else. The statement I hear all the time is, "I can't believe I just told you that. I've never said that out loud before."

In high school, that skill became coveted. I was popular, and I got recognized as a peer leader. I remember this was a highlight of high school, when I identified as a peer leader. The other leaders and I were brought into a separate training where we actually learned how to mediate and work with others around challenges.

So, this is my background. I was always striving for and taking on leadership roles. While a lot of it was because I wanted to manage how other people thought of me, a lot of it was also genuine. There was an aspect of that I liked. I am a very confident person in so many ways, and yet I think it's very powerful to reveal that dichotomy between who I am on the outside versus who I feel like inside, the Survival Self stuff that goes on inside of me. I want others to say, "You too? No!" I want to be vulnerable and show how I've overcome challenges.

Coaching and working with other humans in a learning capacity is my gift. The ability to use my positive lens to make a lasting difference for someone is extremely meaningful to me. The clients I work with have ah-ha moments and transform from there. I've created a shift with many people that will have ripple effects in their lives, moving out to their teams, their peers, and their families. I enable clients to see something they never saw before. I routinely hear, "I didn't realize that's what I was thinking until right this moment. How did you do that?"

My clients feel safe and secure with me and know that I'll always challenge them to step up and out. I don't have to take action from push and burn, stress and pressure. I work from a calm, centered, peaceful place.

Love What You Do, Do What You Love

It was 2013, and I was at the beach with my father. My mom was sick and couldn't be there, but my dad had come to visit the shore house we rented. I asked him, "So, Dad, when are you going to retire?"

He looked at me as if I had twenty-seven heads. That in and of itself didn't surprise me, but what *did* surprise me is what he said about it: "Why would I retire? I love what I do."

I said, "You do?" I was astonished. I'm not even joking; I felt a jolt in my stomach.

He said, "How did you not know that?" He's a tax attorney.

"Because you were always so stressed when I was growing up!"

"That's just how I'm wired," he said. "I really love what I do. Always have."

I had always believed that you had to stress and struggle to make a nice living, so it was pivotal for me to hear that my father truly loves what he does for a living. It was a paradigm shift. Especially when he said, "And *you* should love what you do too!"

This was the permission I needed, and I hadn't even asked for it. It was at that point I began to consider making a change in my career. It was the first in many steps that led me to where I am today.

I am clear with my children that I want them to love what they choose to do, be great at what they do, and make money at what they do. They don't have to sell their souls to make ends meet. I don't have to have deep conversations with my kids about this stuff, because they see it. They know I love what I do. I celebrate my professional wins with my kids. My daughter asks me constantly, "How's it going with your coaching business? Do you like the people you are working with?" So, I want to be an example of enjoying life and creating flexibility. I want my kids to look at me with a level of pride.

My son, who is now twelve, has some learning differences, and they are starting to have more of an impact as he is getting older. Recently, he was supposed to go to executive function training (for organizational skills), and he was resistant. He didn't want to go and said something that just broke my heart: "I'm already stupid; nothing's going to change me." I had tears in my eyes, of course. But he started crying.

I said, "Do you know that Mommy is smart?" He said, "yes." And I asked, "How do you know?" He said, "You have this business," and gave me other examples. It wasn't even a question.

Then I said, "I struggled in the exact same way as you right now. I had differences. I went for tutoring four or five days a week when I was in fifth grade. I just learn differently, and so do you." Then I said, "I wouldn't have the successful business I do today if I hadn't done some work on my own brain."

My words really got to him. He wound up going to his training, and we've talked a lot about the fact that it's not about his intellect. It's about the way he learns, and we will support him through this challenge. I love being able to say, "Hey, you come from a long line of worriers. You come from a long line of challenges that may have stopped others but will never stop us. We don't stop. We create what we love."

You're So Much Closer to Everything You Want Than You Realize

I chose a career in working with other people because I knew that's where my gifts lay. As I said, I was a coach before I stepped into coach training. Coach training simply refined and up-leveled my skills.

Early on in my career, I had assumed my power was in making people feel good. But my power actually lies in seeing someone else's brilliance and talent and magnificence and reflecting it back to them in a way that they can hear it. And also, being able to reflect where their blind spots are and what's getting in the way.

It's a two-sided thing. When clients start out with me, they're guns a-blazing, so excited. Then we get into unpacking the Survival Self stuff, and it's sticky and icky and yucky. I always say the caterpillar goes into the icky, sticky cocoon before it emerges as a butterfly. It's not all rainbows. It actually needs to *not* be that way. The tough stuff needs to be confronted. When I went through coach training, that was my edge: to be bold, to say the things others were only thinking.

I now say, as many coaches do, "I will serve you; I will not please you. I'm going to say things to you, dear client, that no one else in your life will say to you." They might be seeing it, but they're not saying it because they love you, and they're attached to you. They're attached to the relationship you have.

At times, I have felt ashamed about my deep devotion to my career. I "should" want to disconnect like everyone else seems to want to do. But I simply don't, at least not most days. This is a funny thing to feel shame about, yet it is truly something I've felt the need to hide.

Then, something shifted.

As I was hiking through the breathtaking mountains of Colorado this summer, I realized that most people are not in love (or even "in like)" with their work. I *am* different, and that difference is something I am proud of. Something I have cultivated. Something I have intentionally created to be the very backbone of the work I do in the world. *This* is what I coach others to create for themselves: a new relationship with their career, either their current position and career trajectory or a new career altogether. A career where there's nothing to run from, no rushing to retirement, so that you can finally start to live.

Tough Messages

Have you ever wondered what it's like to be coached? It's not easy. Sometimes, it's not fun. It's my job to ask difficult questions, to challenge the status quo for my clients. To shake them up, to separate them from a story that's no longer working. Here are some examples of the tough questions and messages I sometimes give people:

1. What if you got off the struggle bus?
When I reflect that a client is stuck in struggle and suffering, I have said things such as, "You seem to enjoy the struggle. Like maybe you get something out of that. What's the kick you get from your suffering, from your struggle?"

Gosh, the drama. A lot of my clients will try to enroll me in a story of how hard their current circumstance is, and I am not interested in going there. I will say, "Pull up out of the story and the drama. If there wasn't drama, if there wasn't struggle, *who would you be* in this moment?"

2. I'm going to pause you right here. Is this conversation moving you forward?
My clients will often fight for their side, and then I'll reflect that view of how things "are" by saying: "Here, it feels like there's some defensiveness. I'm wondering what that's about."

I'll say things like, "Your employees are scared of you. They're scared of you. Are you intending for them to be scared of you?"

I was working with Matt again, the CEO I mentioned in Chapter 2, and I've seen so much growth. We've been working together for years. I've seen so much shift in him, allowing himself to cede control to others, to empower them. It is often said about coaches, "You spot it, you got it." With a lot of my clients, I can spot it because I've got it: that same need to control. But Matt has taken his hands off the wheel and dropped the need to micromanage how his employees operate. The result is that business has grown and continues to grow tremendously, quarter after quarter.

Six or seven quarters in, Matt was blowing numbers out of the water again. He said, "I think I'm ready to officially step up my goal."

3. Unwillingness to accept support.

I get a sense that many of my clients don't take any time to stop and acknowledge themselves. They have very little room for their own humanity. And while that sounds like butterflies and unicorns again, refusing to hold space for your own humanity is actually very, very toxic. When you are being led by someone who doesn't have room for their own humanity, you can't possibly expect that they're going to allow you to have *your* own humanity.

Do You Do *Everything*? Stop

When someone complains to me about their spouse, manager, or team member, or they complain about their child, they want me to take their side. I am not interested in doing so. Instead, I will ask my client for the commitment beneath their complaint. That's right. All complaints are on top of a commitment. For example, "My manager doesn't listen to my opinion or reward me for XYZ." The commitment beneath this complaint is to create a relationship with the manager where opinions are heard, or where accomplishments are recognized.

I hear this one all the time from mothers: "I do *everything,* everything in the house. My partner doesn't pitch in or doesn't do half as much, and you know, my kids … blah, blah, blah." Instead of buying in to this, I might say, "Do you understand that you're enrolling your partner in X, Y, and Z? You're enrolling them in your drama, in this story." I'll always say, "Well, how are you training them in behaving that way?" The response is, "I'm not. My partner just doesn't step in." I'll say, "Look. Let's consider some of the things you do around the house. Oh, you do the laundry? So, what if you asked your partner to do it?"

If we are not holding our partner, or leaders, or the people on our team, or our business partners as whole and complete, we often begin to over-function. I've done this with my own husband. I realized I had convinced myself—and him—of this idea that he wasn't capable of some of the things that he was perfectly capable of. And, actually, he *wanted* me to convince him of this idea. He also wanted me to be convinced that he wasn't capable of some of the "mom tasks," like taking the kids to the doctor or filling out forms because he doesn't do them quite as well.

But things have shifted so much in our relationship. He and I are very different, and that's why we're together. Together, we make the partnership whole, and there are certain things he does, and there are certain things I do, and then there are certain times we need to ask each other for support. It's my job to accept and love him as whole and complete.

When I think of myself as broken, needing to be fixed, whatever, I look at the people closest to me and ask, *How are* they *needing to be fixed too?* I put the people I love the most under the microscope. I have done this in all of my other romantic relationships in the past: *What's wrong? What needs to be fixed?* Such a woefully unsatisfying way to go through life.

Feedback Cannot Hurt You

Lately, I've been guiding a client to skip playing the victim and lean in to some of the discomfort he's been feeling regarding social stuff. What I mean by that is I've asked him for some feedback about what is causing distress with his friendships. He's had a few recurring themes, and I think I was able to help him.

I always am surprised (yet, not surprised) how unwilling people are to make an investment in themselves and in their minds. It's absolutely the most important investment you can make, and yet, as a society, we have all of these stories about it: "We can go into debt over education, cars, and houses, but our minds? That's ridiculous!" But beyond that, I recently had a light bulb moment about the way I approach things that makes me stand out. The deal is—and this has always been my thing—I am fiercely courageous about leaning in for feedback and am hungry for development. If ever there were a challenge in a friendship, I would always look to learn what was going on and own *my* side of the street so I could hear the other person's side. I am not scared to be uncomfortable. In fact, I thrive on discomfort because that's where growth happens.

The Life Coach School founder Brooke Castillo's powerful work is just brilliant. She teaches "The Model": that the circumstances in our lives are neutral. It's our thoughts and feelings that determine our actions and results, and we have the power to *change* our thoughts and feelings.[16] If you're curious about this framework, I encourage you to listen to her podcast and join her monthly coaching membership program, "Scholars." Brooke's Model is a simple way of condensing the learnings from so many of the thought leaders in the space of "mind management."

Simply recognizing when something is a circumstance—and that all circumstances are neutral—is a mind-blowing revelation for many of my clients.

Are You Going to MSU?

I went to "MSU" in my mind recently. I was watching my daughter at her finale awards ceremony for cheer camp and she didn't look like her normal happy, bubbly self. So, what did I do? My fear mind, my Survival Self, took over and I started MSU.

MSU = Making Stuff Up

I concocted this story that she was having social angst, she wasn't happy, she regretted trying out for the cheer team … I was going to a place in my mind I'm not proud of. Pretty quickly, I caught myself and was able to manage my mind out of this rabbit hole I'd gone down. My antidote is always to get present, which includes connecting to my body. Taking some deep breaths. Looking around and noticing my environment.

When do YOU go to MSU in your mind? And what do you know to do to get out of it?

As is often the case, none of the stuff I made up in my mind was true. My daughter was simply tired!

Next up: we will examine a third component in Emotional Intelligence and the "how" of following your vision roadmap. Are you worried about setbacks? Don't worry. I've got you.

FROM BROKEN TO WHOLE: EXERCISES

1. People who make decisions and take action from their Golden Self do not spend a lot of time talking or thinking about why circumstances are the way they are or what happened in the past. Instead, they are focused on the present, and what they want to create in the future. They tend to be interested in what works and what does not work in terms of creating favorable results. That's not to say that these people don't experience failure—they do. But they see it more as information instead of a final verdict.

    a. When you accept that you are responsible for your life, your relationships, and all of your results, you are empowered. You always have the freedom to choose the way you want to think and to act.

    b. Write down two or three actions you could take in your life right now that could improve your relationships.

2. Conversely, our Survival Selves tend to be victims. They feel powerless or helpless when a circumstance occurs or another person acts in a way they don't like. They react instead of plan ahead. They over-explain, defend themselves, and tell stories.
   a. Write about one area of your life where you've cast yourself as a victim.
   b. Think about how you could tell the story in more empowered way. Or simply a different way.
3. Closure is the act of being fully present. It is a choice you can make at any moment to release the past and any energy you are carrying around a specific area in your life. Choosing to pursue a feeling of closure often involves forgiveness of ourselves or others, acceptance, and acts of generosity.
   a. Say what has happened without judgment and acknowledge closure just as things are, *and* just as things aren't.
   b. Think through or journal answers to the following questions: What haven't I said about this situation that I still feel I want to say? What will change if I say it? What have I learned from this situation? What can I release?

GOLDEN KEYS

- What stories do you tell about yourself? Are they serving you?
- What are your gifts?
- Continuously creating new habits keeps us growing and evolving into the best versions of ourselves.
- If you don't have that feeling inside you that you call fear, you're not dreaming big enough.
- Setting intentions changes everything.
- Ask yourself: Where in my professional life am I playing safe and small? Settling for the status quo?
- How would your relationships be different if you thought of the other person as whole, complete, and fully capable?

EQ CONNECTION: EMOTIONAL EXPRESSION

The next aspect or competency of emotional intelligence, EQ, that I want to tell you about is emotional expression. According to *The EQ Edge* by Steven J. Stein, PhD and Howard E. Book, MD, emotional expression involves openly expressing feelings both verbally and non-verbally through word choice, tone of voice, volume of speech, facial expressions, and body language. People who are skilled at this aspect of EQ are open and congruent in the emotional messages they convey.[17] Someone who isn't good at this aspect of EQ may, for example, tell you that they are interested in hearing about your day but continuously check their phone while you are talking. This incongruency between what they are saying and doing is confusing and sends mixed messages.

Building this EQ component is an important part of following the New Golden Rule. Living a fully expressed life means communicating our emotions—letting them out to connect with others. When someone comes to us and is emotional, we generally offer them kindness. We hold space for them. But unless we are already following the New Golden Rule, we may fail to do this for ourselves. It's time to treat ourselves better. We often understand this cognitively. It's *practicing* it, coming from the heart, that is the biggest challenge.

I'd like to give you a few more examples of lack of Emotional Expression—the incongruency between what a person is expressing and what they *think* they are expressing. I have a client who had a pretty serious heart attack and was in the hospital for nearly a week. He needed surgery and tons of physical therapy, and when we spoke for the first time after his release, he was talking about the experience of the heart attack as though it had happened to someone else. It was very interesting to me. He was very disconnected in his expression. His expression was more in terms of the impact that his heart attack was having on his family, and the impact that it was having on his business, and his fear that he was going to fall behind. When I checked in with him on how he was feeling about it, he was like, "Oh. Yeah, I mean, it sucks." But there was something missing for me. It was hard for me to put my finger on it.

I asked him if he was mad at himself, or mad at God, or if he was angry at all, just in general. He was so quick to say, no, no, no, he was fine, that I just knew it was likely going to come back to bite him—the emotion of what he had been through. Because he wasn't dealing with it or expressing what was inside of him. He was more likely to express anger than sadness. I find this behavior to be pretty common, especially among men.

A couple of weeks later, he ended up being smacked in the face with a whole host of emotions. We did some work on those emotions and to understand that it was okay to release them, and *important* to release them. It led to more conversation about how he often feels one way and acts another way. He is almost convinced that he feels the way he is acting. I was able to reflect that there are emotions inside of him others can pick up on, even if he sometimes cannot.

Another example of this incongruence in terms of emotional expression is a person who says they are paying attention when you know they are distracted. You're on a video chat, and the person is looking outside of the view of the camera. The particular person I am thinking of here is also famous for forgetting our sessions or being late and apologizing. There is a significant gap in self-awareness and in his emotional expression. He runs into this issue with his business partner as he is extremely fact-based and she is more emotionally focused. As a result, he struggles in that relationship. What we've uncovered is that he indeed has a lot of emotion and, specifically, he has a lot of fear. He has just learned to compartmentalize it and shut it off, which on the outside almost looks like arrogance.

I am also thinking of another client who was moved by something that came up in one of our sessions and started to cry. He felt embarrassed by this, ashamed, and said, "I don't even know why I'm crying about this." What we uncovered, of course, is there were emotions lying beneath the surface that were going unrecognized or being pushed to the side. But they were coming out in other ways. They were coming out in him acting aloof or too busy.

I have some clients who want me to see them in a certain way. They want me to see them in only the best of light. They're not recognizing their own judgments or harsh criticisms of themselves. The reason they need to hide who they really are is they're ashamed of that person. The emotional experience of being with someone like that is you get this feeling of sugary fakeness. This behavior puts up a boundary, a wall. You wonder, *Is this person authentic?* You feel a gap.

Especially nowadays, it's clear that the more vulnerable we are, the more connected people can be to us. In today's workforce, being self-involved, being disconnected from emotions, is no longer effective. For example, I don't know the leader of BP, the oil company behind the tragic accident in the Gulf of Mexico, but my assertion is that he has a heart, and he was just so used to coming at things from his head that he had no idea who he was being through the experience of the oil spill. And that disconnect had tremendous implications for his company and people's response to what had happened.

Dig Deeper—It's No Longer Optional

We do not have the option anymore of putting on airs or of not being connected to our emotions. It is abundantly clear when someone is not emotionally connected. It has an impact. It has a cost. People will come to me because they're having a hard time in relationships; they're noticing certain patterns. And often, at the heart of it, there is a need for them to grow in their emotional expression, to express themselves vulnerably. I worked with this individual, for example, who ran his own business and often had interactions with people who were awkward. Of course, that's going to happen. But he was so fearful of being found out, of people discovering that he wasn't perfect, that he wound up crafting responses to people that were so robotic. I was always pushing him to be more and more vulnerable. But he was always worried about it: "I don't want to put doubt in their minds. I don't want them to question my abilities." I would reflect to him: "*You're* questioning your abilities. What has you thinking you have to be perfect? What has you thinking the other person is perfect?"

Recently, I was working with a client, Julia, who said something amazing. We were talking about our work together, just that it is opening up her eyes to new passion that has been lying beneath the surface. She wants to learn a foreign language; she wants to learn to play the piano; she wants to invest more time and energy working with youth. We did some project design and planned out the steps for learning Spanish. I asked, "What is the experience, three years from now, when you are proficient in speaking Spanish?" She replied, "It will feel masterful. I look at people who speak multiple languages and am in awe." At the end of our session, I commended her for being willing to learn another language and take on the accountability around it. I told her I loved hearing how she saw people who speak another language and said, "What I want to reflect to you is that what you see in them is what's inside you." Julia replied, "As much as I do respect those who play the piano and who speak multiple languages, I want to say to you that you have such gifts. And it's inspiring to see you create a career around them. Your gift of insight is masterful. I watch you extract meaning from things I couldn't even see. Your passion for what you do keeps me in this coaching relationship and keeps me wanting to continue to grow myself."

Interesting note about Julia: she had a habit of rescheduling our appointments multiple times, as in more than three times. So, I made a short video to send to her and said, "I'm not concerned about myself, or the impact on my calendar. But I am concerned about you, and what all this rescheduling means. My assertion is that you've gotten used to prioritizing other people and their needs above yourself and your own needs." I was right about this. Her boss had called a meeting at the last minute and she totally could have stood her ground and said, "I am busy with a prior appointment at that time," but she didn't. Julia went into complete reaction mode and said, "I'll move my coaching session or risk losing it (thanks to my twenty-four hour reschedule policy) because

I am not as important as my boss liking me is." I was able relate to her with respect and also push her to take a look at what was really happening. It created a major breakthrough for Julia. It caused her—when she looked back on her life—to see so many missed opportunities. Times when she had not prioritized herself. This insight created a big shift in her commitment to our work together and in her commitment to herself.

STEP THREE

FOLLOWING THE NEW
GOLDEN RULE ROADMAP

*Hindu teachings set out the world's ages
according to their most central qualities.
Truth is said to define the Golden Age.*

Chapter 6

THE "HOW"

Although the world is full of suffering,
it is also full of the overcoming of it.[18]

–HELEN KELLER

How will you get from here to there?

Who will you be when things go wrong?

A client's "roadmap" is the *how* of the work we do together. As I mentioned in Chapter 4, it includes doing values work by looking at peak experiences (those moments in life when the client feels most alive), vision work (when we ask: "What is your intended result? Where do you want to be and why?"), and thinking about what life will be like when you actualize the vision:

- What becomes possible then?
- How will you feel?
- What will your experience of yourself and life be?

From the answers to these questions, we can create and follow the plan from the future to ensure we are not indulging perceived barriers/blocks. Think of this step as standing in the future and working backward, or reverse engineering something.

Designing projects from the future has us coming from possibility, not probability.

Here are some examples of specific project designs:

1. Building skills around empathy is a project one of my clients is working on. He's gotten feedback that he can be terse. We have to look at how to measure progress, or, "How will we know you've moved the needle in this area?" One thing that is measurable is the amount of feedback he gets on this issue. If a month goes by and he hasn't gotten any feedback, or it switches to positive feedback—"something is different with you"—that's meaningful. He'll also know something has changed when he regularly has a clearer conscience. We also might know if someone asks him for a promotion.

2. Getting a new job. It's more than just getting a new job, however. A new role has to be in alignment with the client's career goals and move her forward. Getting a salary increase is also a common project for many of my clients.

3. Improving communication with their team could be a project design for someone. It could involve providing feedback at work to achieve goals with greater ease, or building overall morale to reduce turnover, for example.

Next, we create a strategy to get there so that the client knows what actions need to be taken in what order. If we don't approach project design in this concrete manner, clients get in their own way with thoughts like: *I don't know how, I'm gonna do it wrong, What if I fail?* or, *I've never done it before, so why would I think I can this time?*

Once we have our milestones identified and they are time-bound (by a certain date and with a specific measure), we look at skill set:

- What skills are needed?
- Which of those skills are present already and which need to be built?
- For those to be built, where do we go to build them?

Sometimes I can help the client build the skill myself and sometimes they need outside resources.

Lastly, we plan rewards along the way. Most of my clients have a dysfunctional relationship with rewarding themselves. They are high achievers and will often tell me, "Achieving my goal is reward enough." This, however, is a recipe for burnout. We are reward-driven creatures. Being rewarded motivates us and keeps us in action. We also need to celebrate our wins, both big and small. If we don't celebrate along the way or celebrate once we reach our goals, what's the point of having goals?

A reward serves as a stake in the ground for the milestone achieved. I set my first big reward when I became a coach at getting hired by four clients at a designated rate. My reward was a standing desk, which was a big investment for me at the time. To this day, I look at that desk with pride. I earned it.

A client of mine, Carlos, had a banner year last year. Yet in January, he was back to a familiar place of fear, saying things like, "What if I don't achieve the same level of success this year? What if my run is over?"

I called him out on forgetting an important step in our process: rewarding himself. Carlos loves watches. He wanted a new high-end watch and had a story about that desire being bad or wrong. We coached around it and he finally empowered his decision to honor his accomplishments with a watch he now proudly wears every day.

I'm always listening to my clients for the things—trips or items they desire—to build in to their project plans. Most people have a weighty story about being "selfish" when they speak about rewards, but it is such a key part of building up and honoring your Golden Self. Do not try to skip it or avoid it.

Commitment to Your Vision

It's totally predictable that my clients, who are all busy people, will become "too busy" at some point. Their commitment to the coaching will wane. So, I ask at the beginning of an engagement, "What is going to get in the way of your commitment? What's going to happen? Are you going to get too busy? Are you going to get confronted? Are you going to decide that you are good enough now and you don't need to continue to develop yourself? Or will you be prioritizing other people over yourself?"

Then I ask, "What do you need me to say to you, or who do you need me to be for you, when that moment inevitably arrives?" People appreciate it, because we all have predictable patterns. For me, mine is to get busy and overwhelmed: "I have so much on my plate!"

Busy is not a leadership competency. Being busy does not mean you are important. Prioritizing development is where power lies.

Once we have the map in place, we coach around what's happening in the client's life in relation to their map—particularly if there are points at which they are struggling to stay on course. We also do a number of different exercises throughout our work together. I love distinguishing cycles and patterns with clients—relationship cycles, stress, Survival Self cycles. The goal is to distill what's predictable and how to interrupt the pattern.

I have more than five hundred exercises in my tool belt at this point and pull out the most appropriate tool based on the client.

- **Area of Life:** They look at major areas of life or business and rate where they are on a scale of one to five and what a five in each area looks like. From there, we create one action per category.
- **Energy (not time) Management:** For planning tomorrow, today
- **Well-being Tracking:** Done throughout the week or month (see the end of Chapter 7 for more information on how to do this)

- **Fifty Accomplishments Exercise:** When a client is struggling with confidence and belief in self, I challenge them to list fifty accomplishments or moments in which they felt a sense of pride, fulfillment, or wholeness.

This is the part of my process where I mess with my clients' thinking, using the New Golden Rule. As we discussed previously in Chapter 1, Patrice was feeling undervalued at work. She knew she was being paid less than her peers, yet her performance had been stellar and she was constantly being pulled in to different projects. Patrice was fearful of asking for a salary increase because, as she said, "Maybe I'm not worth it. My boss may get upset or uncomfortable. The company is tight on funds."

Patrice was allowing her fear to hold her back, and ultimately, the company was suffering as well because her engagement was down. What would you say to her, using the New Golden Rule?

Here is another example: Malcolm was interviewing for a new position he really wanted. However, he was spending so much time trying to package himself in the way he *believed* the employer wanted him to be that he was disconnected from his secret sauce— the thing that made him a stand-out candidate, which was his talent for relationship building. He was actually blocking his ability to develop a genuine relationship because he was convinced there was a "right" way to show up in interviews.

Fortunately, we ultimately discovered in our work together that if he were to get a job based on a false representation of himself, he *and* the employer would be shortchanged.

Emily's Predictable Cycle
(Hint, Reader: you have one too.)

High achievers often grab on to new habits with vigor, from a place of wanting to be exceptional. We want to stand out, be recognized, be in the best shape. Thus, a particular cycle begins. I engaged in this cycle in the past (though it can still creep back in sometimes, even today, if I'm not cognizant of my thinking) in order to get what I craved in childhood, which was acceptance, attention, and my dad's love. My cycle is a reliable process for turning everything into a burden, no matter how much I love it.

Others have their own markers along a cycle, but for me, the following sequence is how it plays out. You may see yourself in these steps, or you may have a totally different cycle. Check in with yourself as you read to see if any of this sounds familiar:

1. Commit to something new from excitement. This "thing" could be yoga, exercise, meditation, a business idea, professional development, a particular activity with kids, a house project, etc.
2. Become hyper-focused on it.
3. Spend a lot of time and energy on it.
4. Feel proud of your commitment and compare yourself to others who are not doing it quite so well or with such intensity. This is the "be better than" part of the circle.
5. Make a "mistake," or fail to do the thing perfectly one time. Beat yourself up, create drama.
6. Try to clean up your mistakes, errors, or imperfections, and feel temporary relief.
7. Obsess over continuing to do your thing the "right way." Filter out role models who have success and joy. Surround yourself with friends who struggle and believe that to struggle is the best way to live.
8. Become exhausted, fantasize about not doing the thing anymore.
9. Become annoyed with the thing. Make the thing the problem. Gossip about the thing. Seek validation by complaining to people who will tell you how bad this thing is.
10. Disengage from the thing, all the while beating yourself up and not fully releasing it. *Voilà*, the thing becomes a burden.

11. Get bored, uncomfortable, look for a new thing.
12. Find a new thing. *This is it!* Start the cycle over again.

I encourage people to look closely at this cycle to understand its benefits and its costs. Look at the gifts of what this cycle brings: variety, excitement, engagement. Look at what it costs you as well. Interrupt the cycle by asking yourself, *What would someone who is not in this kind of cycle do? What would Oprah do? What would Michelle Obama do?*

Choose Your Words Carefully

The words you choose to think and speak create your experience of life and the experience others have of you. A few simple examples:

1. We *hope* to solve the problem.
   - We are committed to solving the problem.
2. I *have to* work on that project.
   - I could work on that project.
3. I *should be* networking to build relationships for my career development.
   - I get to network to build relationships for my career development.

"Good Enough" Work

I recently had a super-productive morning. From the time the kids got out the door at about 8:30 a.m. until about 1 p.m., I had my peak productivity hours, and it's important that, even now, I remind myself that this time frame naturally works so well for me. During that particular morning, I set myself up for success by carving out those hours and making sure I would be undistracted. I needed to prepare for a workshop. I gave myself a set amount of time to work on the agenda.

I could have sat and perfected the agenda for hours, but I only allowed myself a portion of that time frame for that task. I said to myself, *It's only going to be a good-enough product today; I'll perfect it over the next couple of weeks because I'll have some time later on.* I knew it wouldn't be perfect, but I got something down on paper, which was great. Then, I spent thirty minutes creating a handout and another fifteen minutes finding someone to design the handout for me on Fiverr, a website specializing in freelance work. I got my freelance hire everything he needed, and by 11:30 a.m., that project was well on its way and I got to take my yoga class—which then fueled me for the rest of the day in my sessions with clients.

I want to highlight the power of good-enough work and surrendering the need for perfection. As many coaches have noted, whatever you make is going to take as long as you give yourself to make it. So, I'm working with several clients right now on constraining the amount of time they actually give themselves.

Active and Passive Development

Leadership skills are highly sought after by employers, and that's because they're rarer than you may think. Leadership is *challenging*. It's part science and part art. The science can be learned conventionally. The art is learned by experience. The ability to combine both separates the great leaders from the rest.

Today's business environment is rapidly changing. This is creating a great demand for those with leadership skills, particularly as it relates to leading others through change. In the past, managers were tasked with maintaining what was working. This is no longer true. If you can lead others through change, you possess one of the most valuable workplace skills—which is why I hope your Golden Self Roadmap includes places to continuously develop your leadership skills.

Leaders have the ability to change companies and the world. Leadership skills are highly learnable and always valuable. Advancing your skills may be the best way to advance your career.

If you've always wanted to become an effective leader, you're in luck. There has never been a better time to enhance your ability to lead others, because there are more opportunities to learn these skills than ever before.

I believe there are two types of development: passive development and active development. Both are important and require focus to become the best version of yourself. Passive development activities for growing your leadership skills include listening to podcasts, reading books on leadership, taking training courses, watching TED Talks, etc. This type of growth leads to incremental shifts. Active development, which leads to transformational and accelerated growth, includes 1) individual and/or group coaching, 2) experiential learning, 3) hands-on exercises, and 4) taking risks in real life.

As you round out this final step, be sure to include plans for your own ongoing development, even if it's as simple as sitting poolside with a book or listening to a podcast while taking a long walk.

Dare Yourself to Exercise

In the month of June 2019, I challenged myself to regularly try new things and step outside my comfort zone. I wore a shredded T-shirt one day that I normally would not have worn to my daughter's school; I asked for help when I normally wouldn't have done so; I sat in silence longer than I was used to with my clients. Here's what I learned (or relearned): My brain tells me to avoid things that will result in negative emotions. Things where I risk failure. My brain is conditioned to see what's wrong. My brain recycles thoughts that create self-doubt and anxiety. Though these recycled thoughts don't move me forward, they are oddly comfortable in their predictability.

When I was willing to feel failure, disappointment, and fear by doing uncomfortable things, my heart would pound, my palms would get sweaty, and then, after some deep breathing ... I'd survive! I'm pleased to report that I created breakthroughs in *every* area of my life that month. And they keep coming!

Where are you shortchanging self-confidence for the illusion of safety, security, and consistency? Are you finally ready to start living a bigger life? Again, everything you want is *much* closer than you realize.

Accountability

You've probably heard the quote, attributed to many different people, "We tend to overestimate what we can do in a day and underestimate what we can do in a year." It's so true and important to remember.

The whole concept of having an accountability partner is a powerful one. It is one of the most effective support structures to get someone into action. If someone knows another human is expecting something of them, this person will get into action. I want to be clear that accountability is more important at the beginning of someone's transformation process; the ideal goal is that we are not overly dependent on any one accountability partner as the source of our creating the shifts and changes we seek. Often, we underestimate the power of our community and of the people in our lives who want to see us win.

What often comes up in conversation about accountability is one's relationship to support. I like to help my clients look at this relationship. Most of my clients tell me they have a hard time asking for support. I can see that because of the way they've set their lives up. There are some exercises I ask my clients to do in which they have to go out and interview people to learn more about themselves, their gifts, perhaps their blind spots. This is during the early part of my process, when clients are working to identify aspects of their Golden Selves. At this stage, I often hear things like, "I don't want to bother people. I'll annoy them. That's presumptuous. They're going to feel forced to say something nice that they don't really believe." But the bottom line is most of us do love to help others. We love to be able to make a difference for others, and yet there's this common belief regarding asking for support for ourselves: *We should be able to do it ourselves; or, We don't want to be a bother.* We somehow got the message that if we have to ask for support, it means we are weak.

You will only get so far if you are unwilling or unable to pull in accountability, support, and the like. That said, I do not believe you want a coach to be your sole accountability buddy. When someone works with me, for example, when we have completed our work together, my intention is that this person is able to launch and leverage accountability in other ways. So, if people ask me to hold them accountable for something, I will often ask why they are automatically turning to me. Is there anyone else in their life who can do so? We will often explore who else is in their life, and discuss the client's relationship to accountability through others. Some people don't want to be held accountable by anyone else because they are fearful that if they don't achieve the results they've set out to achieve or complete that task they said they'd complete, they'll be embarrassed.

So, the picture on accountability is when people commit to something, we find out 1) Are they accountable to themselves, and reliable? 2) If they're not sure, or if they know they're not, who can be their accountability partner? 3) What does accountability look like if their partner or source is not a person?

Setbacks: Progress Doesn't Occur in Straight Lines

Throughout the coaching process, whether you are working with myself or another coach, there are going to be setbacks. These setbacks can occur at any stage of the coaching process: when we are engaged in the Archaeological Dig to find our Golden Selves, when we are working hard to distinguish Survival Self, or while we are in the midst of creating a vision for the next phase of our lives. There are going to be days when progress feels difficult or impossible. It's just part of growing.

I am uniquely able to speak to this topic of handling setbacks due to my health issues. The way I sometimes feel physically is a perfect example of a setback I have to overcome. I often experience, on a deep level, the vulnerability of the body I have.

To help my clients navigate their own setbacks, we build a safety plan in order to handle the inevitable:

- You'll fail.
- You'll talk about something and not do it.
- You'll fall out of integrity with your Golden Self.
- You'll break promises to yourself.

These are all things that may feel compelling enough to take you off course or lead you to abandon your commitment to that future vision. As you face the inevitable discomfort of things getting messy, we want to call these challenges out.

By looking at setbacks head on, I find the people I'm working with aren't often surprised by what they can expect to face. They can then handle any setbacks swiftly without getting off track.

Compare and Despair

All of us compare and despair at different times, some of us more than others. When you look to other people and compare your life to theirs, your career to theirs, your level of happiness to theirs, you are robbing yourself of joy. It's so easy to idealize what's going on for someone else, what's going on over there on the other side of the street. But, of course, you don't know the whole story. You *never* know.

You have one responsibility when it comes to your own satisfaction, joy, happiness, leadership, and that is yourself. I speak to a lot of people. I hear what is working in their lives and what is not. This "compare and despair" trap is so common because we live in a culture that breeds it. You go on to social media, and it is such a trigger for this habit. Do not let comparison rob you of joy. We all have special gifts. My gifts are different than yours. Honor *your* gifts and spend less time comparing, and I assure you there will be more joy.

This topic recently came up for me when I visited Las Vegas to celebrate a dear friend's fiftieth birthday. My inner critic was screaming loudly in my ear at one point during the trip. Maybe you can relate and if so, maybe you will appreciate that you're not alone. Everywhere I went on that vacation, I found myself sucked into a game of compare and despair:

I don't look as good as her.

I'm not as smart as her.

I'm not as successful as her.

I don't have as many friends as that person.

I need time by myself on trips like this. No one else seems to. *What's wrong with me?*

I don't feel well [because of pain and discomfort from my chronic condition]. Why can't I be healthy like others? This sucks.

My kids aren't doing as well as that person's kids. I'm not as good a mom as I should be.

After spelling it out like this, it became clear to me why I was feeling exhausted! The experience I was having there wasn't new to me. It was very familiar, in fact. I felt sick and tired of it.

So, I reminded myself that I knew how to move myself out of that shitty conversation in my head. I'd done it before. I'd written about it, for damn sake! But for some reason, during that trip to Vegas, I allowed myself back in to a cycle of measuring myself against all the external "schtuff" out there. I forgot I simply had a choice.

I needed to remind myself of my greatness. I needed to acknowledge myself for who I am relative to *me*, no one else. I needed to remember all I have persevered through in this life, from a severe spinal deformity that left doctors baffled and unsure how to treat me in my early years, to nearly losing my mother when I was fifteen, to raising two kids with Tourette Syndrome, to building a six-figure business I'm growing with more ease than I ever imagined—all while maintaining a chaotic house with two dogs, a loving marriage to a man who would do anything for me, *and* living with a degenerative and chronic neurological condition … while writing a book.

What I looked like in comparison to someone else in Las Vegas means nothing. That day, I reminded myself: *I am enough. I am proud of myself. I love myself. I can choose how I relate to me, and I choose love.*

From there, I went off to spend some quality time with dear friends. Instead of comparing myself to them, I spent the rest of the trip acknowledging their superpowers and beauty.

Chronic Illness

My own experience with chronic illness is something I can draw from when working with clients who are facing setbacks. My physical limitations have me constantly negotiating the space between *I have so much more to give* and more value to offer to others, with the reality that I have to tap into my own self-compassion and take myself out of the game when I'm not feeling well.

When I am having a bad day, health-wise, I experience tremendous pressure in my head. It feels like my neck is tied up like a balloon, like a vice on my left side. There is a throbbing pressure. It's something I experience weekly or biweekly for the entire day or sometimes just for a few hours. Like many people who feel changes in pressure the way I do, I can usually sense rain coming. I don't like medicines; I don't like how they make me feel. I take the bare minimum. The side effects are not worth it for me. For me, to be clear of mind is critical.

When I'm having an "off" day, my Survival Self says, *Push through it. Suck it up.* I'm still working to dismantle the story I tell myself about needing to be secretive about my health. My concern is that if I'm honest about needing to take a day off here and there, people won't trust me. But when I choose to be secretive, it's like shutting a part of myself down.

When I have days with quite a bit of pressure in my head, I think, *Do I cancel my afternoon?* My immediate Survival Self usually responds to this with something like, *These clients aren't going to trust my word if I cancel. We had a commitment.*

Being honest about my health is something with which I'm currently grappling. My intention in sharing this with you here is to help us all have more honest conversations about our setbacks, our limitations, our own humanity.

What can I do? For me, a lot of times, I just have to shift my mindset from "either, or" to "both, and." I ask myself, *How can I create those same emotional experiences with my clients, even when I am feeling poorly? Would it be possible to still engage with them in a helpful manner? How can I create ease?*

I generally find if I can just get clear about where I am and what I can do with ease, it is possible to move through my day and be kind to myself. *All I need to do is show up.* Powerfully hearing and connecting with my clients is enough. I do not have to go run a marathon with them to be of service. Yet some days, I have to cancel. And that is okay.

My experience with this internal conflict is, again, a work in progress. This is something I get coached on from my own coach. There are times I've shown up when I'm not feeling great. But I think I've learned from those experiences. For the A-type personality like myself, navigating a health challenge is a vulnerable position to be in. I feel a lot of fear around this. The challenge is how to manage my Survival Self around the unknown of what tomorrow will bring. My antidote to that fear—and I have to build muscle around this—is: *Trust in myself and trust in the divine. In God, in the Universe, in Source. I will be okay; it will be okay.*

The Productivity Addiction

My husband is very patient when it comes to my Type A personality and high-achiever habits. He's often the one who picks up our kids, helps them with homework, and makes dinner as I build my business. On a recent evening, it was after 10 p.m. by the time I came out of my work cocoon and shut my computer down. While I felt extremely good about all the items I had completed (is there anything better than a completed to-do list?), the reality of how I'd actually spent the entire evening soon confronted me. My kids were asleep in our bedroom cuddled up next to my husband, who was watching TV. "They were waiting for you," he said, sounding weary. "They wanted to say goodnight but couldn't wait up."

I felt ashamed. It didn't help when I noticed my husband's expression, which was one of disappointment. I had put my addiction to productivity and to checking items off my list ahead of family time—ahead of even saying goodnight to our kids.

I met with my coach the next day and explained what had happened, as well as my feelings of guilt. She didn't try to make me feel better. On the contrary, she said, "You're in a dangerous cycle. We all have a need for connection and acknowledgment of our efforts, but you're putting a need to produce results over true connection with the ones you love the most."

I'm not the only one who loves filling my days to the max, of course. I coach my clients on this same tendency. It's often what we believe is expected of us—or it's what we believe is the one path to "success." But our productivity addiction also causes struggle and conflict with the people we care about. The ones who need us to have some down time, to be present with them during non-work hours.

The thing is, of course, it is so easy to get wrapped up in the idea of "life hacking." Also, we get praised for extreme productivity. Because of this, many of us use productivity as a way to determine self-worth. We're going for that gold star every day, yet it's a slippery slope when your identity becomes attached to (or dependent upon) the opinions of other people.

I had to ask myself, *How would I spend my time each day if I could truly believe I am enough just as I am (and just as I am not)?*

Productivity Attack

Ever had a productivity attack? It's a close cousin to a panic attack. I had such an attack recently, during a span of time in which I hadn't been very productive. That day, I had a full day of client meetings scheduled, but a number of my clients just didn't show. Part of the issue was the day itself—it was the day after the long holiday weekend. These cancellations left me with some space in my schedule, which was great because my family had a new puppy to take care of at the time. I ended up still being busy that day, but I hadn't felt productive. I noticed the old familiar Survival Self emotions coming up for me.

So, in the early mornings and evenings, I did my thought work and journaling at a more rigorous pace. I had to ask myself what my value is if I'm not producing. In the midst of all of that, I developed a migraine during the same time I had another client meeting scheduled. I did not cancel it because I felt I could manage. But I wondered, before the client did actually arrive for our session that evening, *How successful am I going to be? How productive are we going to be together?* I also had this fear, *What if tomorrow isn't productive either? What if I still have this lingering headache?*

It is crazy what my brain tells itself sometimes, tying my value to what I am producing.

Take a Look at Your Own Addiction to Productivity

How we feel about ourselves is often dependent upon the voice in our minds telling us how we *should* act and what we *should* do. When we don't examine this voice, it can tear down our self-worth. Building a resilient identity not based on productivity or the opinions of others is a muscle that we build over time. Here are some ways to do so:

1. Ask, *Am I setting productivity goals because I believe I need to be fixed?* Stop giving this inner voice all your power. Once you do, you'll create the time and space to get some clarity about what you really want personally and professionally. The idea is simple: instead of being addicted to the praise of others for your hard work, you alone set the direction for what you do next. *That's* living under the New Golden Rule.

2. Spend some time each morning identifying the top two things you want to accomplish each day. Then structure your day to do these two items. While you'll certainly have the urge to do more, especially at first, practice slowing down. Notice that the world doesn't fall apart.

Jumping off of the productivity hamster wheel takes hard work and dedication, yet every area of your life can be improved by your increased awareness of why you're focusing on productivity.

When you take ownership of the habitual ways you think about your career and life, the payoff is enormous. I recently heard this insight from a client of mine in the wake of some work we did on this area: "I can stop trying to make up for lost time in my past because none of the time was actually lost. It all led me to where I am today. This gives me breathing room to enjoy the moment."

YES.

It's Not All or Nothing

I mentioned earlier that I recently went on vacation with my family to Colorado. It was amazing. I worked for a bit each day, hands-on with clients, getting coached myself, and taking care of back-office stuff. Yep, I went on vacation, *and* I worked. *And* I'm a coach who coaches high performing humans who struggle to unplug from work to enjoy their life. And here I am modeling *working while on vacation.*

Here's the difference between me and most of the people I serve when we first start working together:

- I *chose* to remain partly plugged in, and I have learned the art of shutting off when it's time to be present, connect to loved ones, and relax.
- I have created a lifestyle business that I don't have (or want) to run away from in order to breathe. Well-being is a part of my daily life and a mandate in order for my work to be effective. My everyday life probably looks like a vacation to some people.
- I have generated the self-awareness necessary to know my gifts, intuition, and values, and to use all three daily. Energy-wise, this is where I am in what some people call a "flow state" or "in the zone."

Recently, my coach asked me, "What's your greatest gift?" I answered, "Empathy. I can feel my clients' emotions so strongly and so clearly that sometimes I am aware of them even before they are." He then asked what the dark side of my gift is. I took a few moments and then replied, "At times, I've allowed my empathy to hold me back from saying what I see in my clients' blind spots. I refrain from saying the bold and often disruptive reflection that could make the biggest difference, the one thing that could serve my clients at the highest level, the thing that no one else in their life will say to them."

And just like that, something shifted inside me.

In order for me to share my greatest gift more generously, I must take more risks, get more uncomfortable, and say with more assurance what needs to be said, even when I'm scared. I don't need to be "productive." I need to be authentically me. I need to meet my own needs using the power of the New Golden Rule.

Find the Gifts

My challenge to any individual dealing with any kind of setback is to find the gifts that setback might offer. I hear these types of setbacks a lot: "My company got sold," "We lost a major customer," or "I didn't get that job I thought I was going to get." What was something positive that came from such a difficult situation?

In conversation with the client, my goal is to help them get to a place where they can be with the setback—whatever it may be—as opposed to arguing with reality. I want them to be reflective and move forward, but I do understand that people need space to process their emotions. I want to acknowledge difficult circumstances without wallowing in them.

I have a client, for example, who recently lost a family member she was very close to. She is building a business, and this loss has thrown her for a loop. It's slowed her process down, and I know this slowdown is creating fear for her. My role in helping her navigate this painful transition is not to serve as her emotional support system. She has friends and family for that. With me, she got clear on what's going to matter most to her on her own deathbed. The gift we discovered in this setback is that she spent time with her dear family member in her final hours, which gave her a great sense of peace.

During a client setback, whether it's a death in the family, a health issue, or a job loss, I'm very careful to not play into the "woe is me" victim mentality. Sometimes I need to check my heart at the door a bit because how I might naturally feel regarding my client's setback truly doesn't serve my client.

I encourage my clients to feel their sadness or anger on purpose. If you've got deep emotions coming up, find a way to process them. You can break plates, rip up paper, sit down with a sad movie and cry—get your body into it.

Anxiety

I have an anxious brain. I always have. Over the past few years, thanks to coaching and healing modalities, I've had weeks where I've all but forgotten about my anxiety. I've found a calm and stillness deep inside that I never imagined existed. However, on a recent Sunday during a holiday weekend, that old familiar feeling of anxiety was bubbling up for me, barking about a long list of to-dos, shoulds, and musts. It was also harshly criticizing me for my desire to relax, take a break, recharge my battery. Do you relate? Anxiety is one of the most common setbacks faced by my clients as they work to live into the New Golden Rule.

On days like that one, I reach for a few trusted practices I've cultivated:

- I remind myself how far I've come and that anxiety is nothing to be afraid of. There's no emotion I can't handle.
- I breathe deeply.
- I acknowledge that my brain has switched to auto-pilot, falling into an old familiar thought pattern. I can jump into action to check things off my to-do list and seek momentary pleasure (like a hit), *or* I can choose to face my discomfort by, yep, you guessed it, relaxing and connecting with those near and dear to me.
- I do a ten- to twenty-minute guided meditation specifically designed to reduce anxiety.

I often struggled with anxiety during the holidays since the excitement and anticipation this time of year can be particularly challenging for children with special needs and, naturally, their parents. Children are faced with so much stimulation, their impulses are difficult to suppress, schools are closed, and schedule changes throw everyone off.

If you could put down your anxiety and worries about what will be this holiday season (or cut them in half), you would. I do exactly that by setting aside thirty days during this time of year and calling it the "Worry-Free Living Month." I have even encouraged my daughter to do this practice as well. Since eighty-five percent of what we worry about never happens—and even when it does, it's typically not nearly as difficult to handle as we think it will be—we waste a whole lot of time and energy worrying with little return on investment.

During the "Worry-Free Living Month," I am committed to creating a holiday season where we can just be together as a family, being with what is and what is not. Energy once spent trying to change, control, and manage everything is channeled toward gratitude, appreciation, and being in the present moment. Having two children with their own anxieties, I am crystal clear on the fact that staying in my cycle of worry sends the message to my children that this is the way to "do" life. They need to feel, see, hear, and experience something different.

You may be thinking that this all sounds great, but you might worry that it will never work for you. Or, it sounds great, but you can't figure out how to make the change. While there is absolutely no "right" way to go about making this shift, here are the steps I've carved out for myself. The goal here is to reduce some of your worries and this is what I have personally found helpful. If, however, you're finding these things especially difficult to do, I recommend speaking to a professional. You get to decide your path as the ultimate expert in your own life.

1. Worrying is a bad habit. And, like any other habit, forming a new, healthier one requires gaining clarity on the purpose of letting go of the worry.
   - What will life look like without worry? What will dropping the worry make possible that isn't possible today?
   - By writing down the answers to these questions, and revisiting them over the course of the month, you will continue to present yourself with what you truly want.

2. Next, generate awareness around your worry.
   - When does it happen? How do you know when it's happening? What purpose does it serve for you?
   - Becoming mindful of your worry might include writing down every time you have a worried thought or recording the number of times you worry in an hour.
3. From here, create a new habit to replace the worry.
   - Repeat a mantra in your head when the worry creeps in, pick up a small ball and drop it, or state something out loud that you feel grateful for.
   - Maintain your spirituality practice. Connecting to something higher than yourself reminds you to let go and trust.
4. Next, enlist the support of a loved one or friend to keep you accountable.
   - Support can take any form. Your husband, mother, and daughter will all be charged with holding you accountable at your request. Your husband will remind you twice a day in person; your mom will do so over the phone each morning; and your daughter will text at least once a day.
5. Finally, having compassion for yourself when you backslide is going to be of utmost importance. No worrying about worrying allowed![19]

Breaking Through Plateaus

Sometimes, I work with clients who have grown a lot in the past, but they still seem stuck. This is when they come to me for coaching. They don't want to backslide but are getting comfortable before they've arrived at a goal. Here is a situation I hear about often: there hasn't been one defining moment, tragedy, or problematic event in an individual's life; rather, they are experiencing a steady decline in engagement, excitement, connection, or commitment to their career. This can be a result of burnout from not rewarding oneself or acknowledging one's growth. Often, we'll spend time coaching around the ground the client has taken in his life up to this point. Doing so can inject fire into a smoldering pile of ashes.

The other thing that often "wakes the client up" from the plateau or spinout is connecting with their Golden Self. From that place, the clouds part and the sun shines through. Suddenly, new opportunities are illuminated, and the client has renewed engagement. It's critical that I support the client to get into immediate action when this happens.

The plateau can also be evidence of boredom. As humans, we have a need for variety. Sometimes all we need is a change in scenery, a new project, to walk a different way, to infuse renewed energy into life.

Facing Setbacks with a Healthy Dose of EQ

Confession: I woke up in the morning recently with a familiar feeling of despair. My thoughts centered on self-judgment and criticism about the way I had eaten (lots of sweets and candy) the day before, as diet is a critical component of managing my medical condition.

So, what caused me to knowingly eat off my plan?

Unmet needs.

The good news is I could recognize it. The even better news? I knew how to interrupt the cycle so I didn't repeat old disempowering behaviors.

The backstory here is that my family and I had recently gotten our new puppy, and we were up early, in bed late, cleaning up accidents, and adjusting to a new dynamic at home. During all of that, my needs had taken a backseat. That day, I had woken up acutely aware of this change and planned to take a yoga class to give myself quiet, space, and movement. Then, *I didn't go.* I rationalized my decision to skip class: *I'm tired. I'll do YouTube yoga after I nap*. I didn't. Instead, I went for the immediate *feel good* with comfort food.

Understanding your predictable patterns is the first step to shifting a behavior you don't desire for yourself. Unmet needs are often the culprit of bad habits. Self-forgiveness when you falter, because you will, is the second step. Perfectionism has no room here.

And the third step? Get back on the horse, as they say, ASAP. I ended up going to yoga after all on that day—at 4 p.m. Namaste.

EXERCISES FOR FOLLOWING YOUR ROADMAP AND FACING SETBACKS

1. Write down one specific, targeted action for one area of your life. For the action, write what you intend to produce (or do) and how you will measure the success of the creation or action. For example: "My plan is to create an active Instagram account that features my artwork and post six completed art pieces to the new account by March 15, 2021."

2. Write down one or two specific ways that achieving your biggest goal will help others. One client of mine was struggling to complete his training to become a Physician's Assistant. But when we talked through how his program would help him better serve the people in his community who needed him, it changed his thinking, and studying got easier.

3. Identify three tangible results you will enjoy when you reach a specific goal. It's not enough to say you'll "be happy" when you achieve a goal. Think in more concrete terms, such as, *If I complete my PA training and get a good job offer, I will be able to take my mom to Washington, DC to visit the Smithsonian Museums. She will love it.*

4. Build a streak. Jerry Seinfeld famously used this one to make joke-writing a habit: each day he wrote a joke, he was able to make a specific mark on his calendar. He didn't ever want to break his streak, so he kept his joke-writing habit going.

 **GOLDEN KEYS**

- The willingness to make decisions (regardless of how tough they are) is a key leadership differentiator.
- There are challenging things in life, and I am resolute about not letting them get in my way. What are your thoughts about life's challenges?
- When it comes to setbacks and roadblocks, it's not "if" you will experience them, but "when." Make a plan ahead of time for who you will be and what you will do when a challenge presents itself.
- What got you to this level of success was saying "yes." What gets you *there*—to your end goal—is saying "no."

EQ CONNECTION: STRESS TOLERANCE

I'd like to talk about the link between the Survival Self and stress tolerance, because much of the stress reaction is a Survival Self reaction. Pretty much all of it is, actually. The two are definitely tightly tied together. Some people thrive in stressful situations, while some shut down and are not their best selves when stress arrives.

This has been a tremendous area of growth for me. The way my body is built—the deformity in my spine that has the muscles in my shoulders constantly engaged and tense—causes not emotional stress but *physical* stress (from my spine's missing six discs). I came into this world predisposed to stress and anxiety. I mention this physiological aspect because it is just a piece of me. My body is just automatically predisposed to that fight, flight, or freeze response, and this means, no matter what, for the rest of my days, I will need to manage stress in a very proactive way. Because if I am not working on it, it will come back with a vengeance, increase over time, and derail me.

I used to be incredibly reactive. Anything and everything could stress me out and *would* stress me out. When I was in that state, I would give off a vibe of being harried, frenzied, rushed, moving quickly. I know I'm painting a picture here of a crazy woman, and it wasn't that. It was more just that I literally moved fast. In coaching, this energy was reflected to me, and I didn't like it. *And* I didn't know how to change it.

The breakthroughs have come in slowing down. In learning how to breathe. I had my first major breakthroughs in dealing with stress when I started yoga six years ago. It was the first time I was forced to be on my mat. I used to practice for ninety minutes at a time, and for a while, while I was healing myself, I practiced five to six days a week. It was a huge time commitment. But I learned about myself during that time.

It was through that experience that it became abundantly clear that I was, professionally, in the wrong line of work. I would fantasize about what it would be like to have a life like the life I have created for myself today.

Other things I do to manage my stress:

- I sit quietly.
- I go out into my backyard. Nature is a grounding force for me, and I know it is for so many people.
- I ask myself, *Will this matter on my deathbed? Or, in a hundred days? A hundred weeks?*

My Survival Self has me enlisting other people in how hard and bad and challenging life is, and what a victim I am. People love to get on that bandwagon: "It's so hard! Things are so hard!" Commiserating is this immediate hit; it feels good right away. It scratches an itch.

When I feel overwhelmed, I get on the phone with my mom, and she tells me I have every right to be overwhelmed, and that it's so hard and she doesn't know how I do it. In a way, it's like she's stroking my ego, but I wind up feeling the same way or even worse in the end. So, one of the things I have learned to do is to coach the people in my life so they understand that when I show up in a conversation and I am stressed, what I need to hear is, "Hey! You've got this. You've *always* got this." I need to hear that no matter what, I can overcome the odds. Because I always do.

Also, sometimes I need space. One of the things my Survival Self likes to do around stress is to fix the problem. For example, when my daughter was diagnosed with Tourette, I went into massive fix-it mode. I found every bit of information I could. I become singularly focused on solving her problem. Now, I don't actually look at it as a problem. Yes, something is chemically off that shows as involuntary movements or sounds. But when I look at her as whole and complete, that is more empowering. I can ask myself, *Is there something related to her "disorder" that needs attention, that needs work? Is there something she needs some help with or partnership on from me?* But I'm no longer in fix-it mode. When I get scared or stressed, it's easy to go back into that mode, but as soon as I find myself hopping on the computer to do just a little more research, I check myself: *Oh, right. I'm doing it again.*

I still practice yoga two to three days per week. I'm not nearly as devoted to it as I was, but it is a very important part of my life.

I also take ample breaks throughout the day. I have set my business up so that I am able to do that. September is usually insane and has me feeling pressured and stressed, but when that month rolled around recently, I didn't feel that way. At all. In fact, I wondered, *Am I missing something?*

I have created my dream life. I have everything I need right now. It's all by my own creation, and it wouldn't have been possible without getting a hold of my stress first. And the truth is, on the outside, it doesn't look all that different than it did five years ago. But it feels so different on the inside. There's just more connection, more love, more room for everyone's humanity. There's love and support. It's beautiful.

Chapter 7

THE "SELFISH" HABITS OF WELL-BEING, SELF-CONFIDENCE, AND OPTIMISM

The way we can allow ourselves to do what we
need to, no matter what others may say or do,
is to choose love and defy fear.[20]

–Martha Beck

Are you taking care of yourself?

Well-being is the foundation for living your best life. Without it, anything we build or attempt to build is on shaky ground and will fall apart with even the slightest wind gust. Checking in on your well-being is always a part of the coaching process, whether you work with me or with any other skilled coach. It's also, of course, the foundation of the New Golden Rule. Your well-being is in your hands and your hands alone.

Well-being is key to being a good leader. I am very open about my own well-being and health challenges. I strive to be a leader in terms of what it looks like to care for oneself. Many of us who are in leadership roles, whether we are leading our families or a business or doing both, neglect taking care of ourselves. Often, this stems from a little voice in our minds that tells us we are not enough. Or perhaps that we are too much. It tells us we must take care of other people or that we are being rude if we step away for some time to ourselves.

But who am I to show up as a leader, a coach, a powerful woman, if I am not caring for Number One?

Recently, I spent the day in New York City, which is about a two-hour commute from where I live. I enjoyed the day and had several great meetings. But, of course, just being in the city equals energy out. On the way back home, my little voice was telling me, *You have work to do, articles to read, content to create!* Fortunately, because I have an awareness of that voice *and* an awareness of my body, I paused and noticed my body was *screaming*. It was saying, *Close your eyes. Meditate. Relax. Be silent.*

Allow yourself to just *be*.

Not easy for an A-type personality, right? So, I share this with you to say that none of us do self-care perfectly. It's not something to get right. It's simply about honoring yourself. Your care for yourself is the center of everything else you put out into the world.

Recently, I led a workshop for women executives, many of whom were in their late thirties or early sixties. I had them fill out a twenty-four-hour wheel to look at how they routinely spend their time. One woman in particular teared up when she saw how much she was actually working on a typical day. There was no space for community—one of her core values—or for tending to her own health. That's not good.

When I am working with you, we establish a list of well-being basics—those habits that, if not handled daily, weekly, or monthly, cause significant problems. Examples include:
- physical activity
- flossing teeth
- calling a loved one
- balancing checkbook

- date night with partner
- time to focus on a hobby
- meditation
- cooking
- time with friends
- healthy eating
- religious study
- reading
- learning something new

We all have the need for engaging in well-being basics (these or others), and in order to be at an optimal state, we need to create the space in our lives for these things. Some of my clients use a well-being checklist to track their progress. This is always fascinating because we can distinguish patterns by doing this for thirty days.

When a client shows up in breakdown mode—harried and stressed, or resistant and negative—I check in with them on their well-being habits. Often, we can connect the dots to a breakdown via well-being. One thing my chronic health condition has taught me is the power of taking full ownership for how I fuel, care for, nurture, challenge, and preserve my body.

A few days off of my low carb diet, for example, has me looking at my life, myself, and the world differently—and not in a good way.

The link between self-confidence and well-being is strong. Maintaining well-being is a great place to start building confidence. Remember, confidence comes from taking action even when you don't want to and/or are afraid. Confidence is a *result*, not a requirement. We become more self-confident when we make promises to ourselves and keep them—when we stay in action even when we don't "wanna."

Many of my clients say, "I need to be more confident." To that, I ask, "When you are more confident, what will be possible?" I hear things like:

- "I'll ask for a raise."
- "I'll advocate for my point of view in a meeting."
- "I'll let that coworker know I don't agree with his or her approach."

The idea many people have is, *When I get confident, I will take that action.* But they've got it wrong. Confidence, again, comes from taking action and being willing to fail. It's not usually a place you get to first. Anyone you revere as confident is leaning in to fear. These role models feel the fear and move forward anyway. What are you going to take on that you are afraid of?

With most of my clients, self-confidence is often the first major shift they experience in our work together. They are able to find a newfound commitment to themselves through the lens of well-being. Often, the people who come to me have put everyone and everything before themselves. They've gotten into some bad habits in terms of their eating or their exercise routine (or lack thereof). Their spiritual practice. Their ability to unwind, meditate, that kind of thing. It's all abandoned, or barely existing.

When our well-being is well-managed (and I'm not talking managed perfectly, so long as it's a high priority), and we keep promises to ourselves—like getting up early to go to the gym, eating healthy, practicing meditation, whatever the thing is—we feel better. When we feel better, we are more confident. We know we can believe in ourselves when we keep promises to ourselves. When we do not keep promises to ourselves, we build up this story that we can't be trusted, that we've tried before and it never sticks. You see this often with people who start something with vigor and then end up stopping because, for one or two days, they fell off the wagon.

The way that you care for yourself and the level of confidence you have in yourself are very, very tightly linked. I often can get a good read on someone's self-confidence based on how well they are taking care of themselves. When most people come to me, their well-being is off. The foundation is shaky; everything is off. Once a person has a breakthrough in well-being practices—for example, they exercise three times per week for two weeks—things really start to shift in regard to confidence.

I did a lot of work with my client, Patrice, around well-being and confidence to support her in asking for her raise. Asking for a raise requires courage. If you request a raise while your confidence is down, it's obvious. You are not as likely to succeed in getting what you want.

I've seen clients shift dramatically in this manner, and what's cool is that confidence is exponential. Confidence breeds more confidence. I have a client I've been working with for years, Jennifer. Her heart was really protected when we first started working together. She was constantly protecting herself from being judged. The way she came across to others was as quite judgmental, ironically. She has really been able to break up that context and has become so much more open-hearted, both through the practices we've created for her, and through the deep work she's done on herself. Because she feels more confident now, she behaves with more empathy toward others.

Over-Apologizing

Another bad habit I see often among my clients who struggle with confidence is over-apologizing. This is a very disempowering habit that gets in the way of well-being.

Do you have a habit of apologizing too much? It is possible you do and may not even realize it. While heartfelt apologies can be healing and powerful when appropriate, if you notice that you're apologizing each time you ask to see a menu or bump into a chair, it's time to work on cutting back. I'll be the first to acknowledge that it's tricky to strike the right balance when it comes to apologies. After all, taking responsibility for your actions and making amends shows you have solid character and strengthens your relationships. However, when saying you're sorry becomes excessive, you could be undermining your own power. It is important to learn where to draw the line so you can express remorse without feeling guilty for things that are insignificant or beyond your control.

So, how do you become more aware of your behavior and find alternatives to apologizing? Here are some ideas to try:

1. **Slow down.** Take a deep breath before you blurt out an apology. Give yourself time to think about what you want to say instead of operating on autopilot.

2. **Check your motives.** You might be trying to gain security or appear agreeable. You might even be pretending you're sorry so you won't have to listen to the other person's point of view. In any case, check to see if you're really remorseful.

3. **Change your habits.** Maybe there's something about your lifestyle that you need to confront. Are you often contrite after shopping binges or losing your temper?

4. **Keep a journal.** Writing about your day can help you to notice your triggers and explore your emotions. Jot down what's happening and how you feel when you apologize needlessly.

5. **Lighten up.** Anxiety can make you prone to apologizing. Find relaxation practices that work for you such as meditation or physical exercise.

6. **Reach out for support.** If you're not sure if you're going overboard, ask your friends and family for feedback. They can also support you while you're trying to change. If you think you need more assistance, you may want to talk with a professional coach or therapist.

Now that you're ready to apologize less, you can experiment with different approaches. You may even find yourself picking up new communication skills. Try out some of these alternative strategies:

- **Express gratitude.** Saying "thank you" is often a more logical alternative to saying you're sorry. Plus, it will probably make the other person feel better too. For example, thank a salesperson for suggesting an item that's on sale instead of apologizing for not noticing it yourself.
- **Show compassion.** Saying you're sorry about the misfortunes of others can just be a form of expression. However, if it makes you feel guilty for things that are beyond your control, you may want to phrase it differently.
- **Be direct.** Ask a question without apologizing first. It's reasonable for you to clarify the details of an assignment at work or check the directions to a party. You'll get the answers in less time, and you may be treated with more respect.
- **Accept yourself.** Maybe you wish you had curly hair or a deeper voice. If you can learn to laugh at your more unusual qualities or just feel comfortable with them, you'll feel less need to make excuses for them.
- **Assert your needs.** The biggest downside to excessive apologizing is that it may reinforce the idea that you're unworthy of love and respect.

Build up your confidence with positive affirmations and worthwhile achievements so you can be comfortable and competent with advocating for yourself. Save your apologies for the times when you're sincerely remorseful and have done something you need to make amends for. You'll feel more confident about yourself, and your words will be more meaningful.

Optimism is a Muscle–Work It!

Optimism ties in here too. First and foremost, in order to create any new habit (and that's what we're talking about here with well-being) we must *hold a belief that it is possible.* If we are dragging around our past failings and *I've never done that before, so I can't do it now* types of thoughts and attitudes into our present lives, we'll prove ourselves right.

Now, don't mistake my meaning here. I'm not saying we should fool ourselves into believing it'll be easy. *That's* certainly not realistic. Optimism is a skill that usually must be learned. My low-optimism clients tell me they don't want to view the world with rose-colored glasses. They try to look at what might not work in a situation so they aren't disappointed in the future. But I tell them that optimistic people are happier people. And it makes sense. Our thoughts create the life we believe we have.

I recently met with a client who had experienced a major accomplishment at work the previous week. She was proud, energized, and feeling good. I asked her to share with me the breakthrough she experienced with this accomplishment. She said, "It gave me an inflection point to remember to savor the moment now. I will never have this exact experience again." I got the chills. Such powerful words.

The reality about optimism is that we all face setbacks and disappointments. The ability to recover and claim a happy state is connected to a person's optimism. So, being optimistic and hopeful most of the time really does make a difference in someone's general sense of happiness.

Questions I'll ask when I'm working with people around this idea include, "Where are you least optimistic? How could this situation be improved?" Or, "When you are faced with a new challenge, how do you typically feel?" My client and I might look at emotions and ask why they may feel this way. We are connecting the emotions to what has them thinking certain thoughts.

If you want to be more optimistic, you have to make an intentional choice to look for what is positive. Practice gratitude. Acknowledge the miracle of you being here on this planet and getting up every day. It's amazing.

People who are lacking in optimism tend to defer to a "victim" way of looking at life. What do I mean by that? Victims are not particularly interested in experiencing a radical change for the better in their lives; they focus on what other people are doing instead of how they can move the needle for themselves over time. Victims love a quick fix. They tend to make excuses or find reasons a course of action won't work. They run from discomfort. They like other people who will agree with them about how bad things have gotten.

Here are some other signs you might be sliding into victim mode in your life:

- You seek a lot of advice instead of tuning in to inner wisdom or trusting yourself to take action.
- You are looking to be rescued.
- You believe your interpretation of a situation is the truth.
- You have "a lot of problems."
- You are dramatic.

The concept of, "it's all bad news out there; therefore, I can't be happy," is a victim approach. I'm not saying there's no challenging news out there. But you get a say as to what you tune in to. I personally don't listen to the news much. I read the headlines and am in the know to the extent I find is healthy for me. I tune out a lot of the negative noise that I've noticed generates feelings of helplessness. I want to be very clear, though: this does not mean I don't advocate for the causes I believe in or that I don't work hard to bring positivity into the world or make changes. But what I find regarding pessimism is that misery loves company. And that's not the kind of company I want to be in.

Often, when a client works with me and experiences a transformation, I hear about how hard it can then become for this person to be with the people who he or she now recognizes are so negative. So much of optimism comes from surrounding yourself with people who are likewise committed to seeing things optimistically. Seeing that there are possibilities. That we are not helpless. If we fall into a negative mindset, we often abdicate personal responsibility for making a change or from making the world a better place. I do not tolerate such stances with my clients and in my own life.

Caitlin is one of my executive clients who used to be so pessimistic. She heard some rumblings at work, and she would automatically think the worst. She would play out these scenarios in her head and go right into her Survival Self. She protected herself in these conversations she would have in her head. She would completely make stuff up! We were able to separate who she is from the stories in her head. She was able to get clear about what she really wanted out of a certain situation, how she wanted to view it versus how she was viewing it, and that she had a choice. Things really shifted for Caitlin. She has become the go-to person in her organization for being everyone else's cheerleader. She's much more positive, and she cares for herself. She's far less likely to go to that automatic place now of toxic negativity.

I was just working on this topic with a new client last month, and she said, "If I could become more optimistic, I think I'd see new possibilities, new potential work opportunities for myself. But right now, I'm so stuck in going to the negative that I can't even see what might be possible because I'm blocked."

Bingo.

Get a Coach Already!

No discussion of self-confidence, well-being, and optimism is complete without mentioning the obvious: *get a coach*. You deserve it. Coaching is a higher-level conversation intended to look at the bigger picture, your greater professional "what for."

As a coach, I ask thought-provoking questions intended to get you out of your own way. I am trained to see and hear what's in your blind spot and reflect it back to you. From new awareness, you and I co-develop actions intended to create lasting shifts. Here are the biggest reasons why it's time for you to get serious about hiring a master coach:

1. **Gain clarity around what YOU want.** Sometimes the hardest step is the first step. What do you want from your career? Where do you want to be in five, ten, fifteen years? What will become available for you when you hit those milestones? A skilled career coach draws the conversation to a higher elevation to provide you with clarity around what *you* really want, distinguishing your true desires from what your family, company, friends, and community want for you. All too often, people jump straight into action when they discover a fork in the road with their career. Sadly, this typically results in meeting the same frustration down the road with your next job.

2. **Keep it real.** Everyone goes through periods when they ask themselves if they are in the right job or profession. It's normal to have questions. After all, most of us spend more of our lives working than doing anything else. Working with a career coach supports you in determining whether a career pivot is really what you're after. There are times a client will come to me for a career change only to learn that what they actually need is a change in another area of their life.

3. **Get support and accountability.** A career coach wants you to succeed; your coach got into this line of work to be of service to others. Support and accountability are a big part of what makes coaching so successful. Just like your personal trainer at the gym who holds you to your commitment to build muscle and trim fat because you said that's what you want, your career coach will hold you to the plans, milestones, and actions you have created together. This will often reinvent your relationship to

support structures, guiding you to lean on people in your life and resources you typically do not rely on.

4. **Hold up the mirror.** Have you ever practiced a speech in front of a mirror or tried on an outfit before a big event and noticed something you didn't realize was there? A nervous laugh, or static cling on your skirt? Consider a coach to be a mirror reflecting back to you what's in your blind spot, those limiting beliefs you can't see or that you hold as truths, or those mindset traps that have you engaging in self-sabotaging behaviors.

5. **Own your career.** Your career is yours to own. Too often, we find ourselves feeling like we are solely at the mercy of a difficult boss, a challenging culture, endless piles of work, or long hours. Settling into the position of victim is all too easy. A career coach will continue to stand for you by reminding you to be responsible for yourself and your goals, and to create what you truly desire.

6. **Live into possibility.** As my daughter says, "Anything is possible." A well-trained coach will not buy in to the limiting stories you've created about your career and capabilities. Look for a coach who has created breakthroughs in what's possible in her own life. A courageous coach will best support you through your inevitable breakthroughs.

When Life Happens, Who Will You Be?

During my yoga practice recently, my teacher Jess shared something that got me thinking. She said that at the end of her pregnancy with her twins, she was up eighty pounds and feeling out of sorts with her body. Then Jess's friend, whom I assumed was another yogi, commented on how wonderful her transformation was. Jess must have been dumbfounded by her friend's comment. What could be great about all this weight gain? About feeling like her body was alien to her? About knowing what lay ahead to get back in shape once she gave birth? Jess's friend explained further. She said that now Jess had the gift of understanding her ill, overweight, and out-of-shape students in a new and profound way because she herself had experienced something similar.

Looking at Jess today, you'd never know what she went through. When she teaches, though, she shares her experiences and relates to all of her students from a place of connection, no matter where they are with their practice, their body, or their mind. It hit me that this level of empathy and ability to support her students through the practice of yoga is possible *because of* Jess's journey, not in spite of it. No training or book could have prepared Jess the way personal experience did.

So why do I share this story? Because I see my own journey in that of my teacher.

In June of 2010, my then five-year-old daughter was diagnosed with Tourette Syndrome, as I've mentioned throughout the book. The diagnosis came after months of desperately trying to figure out what was going on with her. The months leading up to the diagnosis were filled with doctor's visits, conversations with other parents, reading books, and, of course, many Google searches on tics, anxiety, rage disorder, neurologists, vitamin regiments, dietary changes, and on and on.

I felt alone, petrified of the future, dreading the diagnosis I was pretty sure we'd be getting. Spending time with my daughter, something I had once longed for as a working mom, became a source of stress for me. I struggled to be in the moment with her. How could I focus on the board game we were playing when her eyes were rolling, her head dragging to the side, her hands stretching and clenching rhythmically? How could there be any simple pleasures when my little girl's brain was "malfunctioning"?

When I wasn't with her, I worried, *How was she feeling? Were other kids making fun of her? What did it feel like to experience tics all the time? What did other parents think? What were her teachers saying?*

And then came the blame game, the one where I decided this was all my fault. After all, I had carried her for nine months. I'd had a hard time with my fluctuating hormones, vomiting through the bulk of my pregnancy. I allowed the stress of my job to get to me during her gestation and early in her life. Maybe living on milkshakes and bagels while pregnant (it was all I thought I could tolerate) had caused this. Or perhaps it was the medications I took during my pregnancy for the nausea and other symptoms. The doctors had said these medications were safe, but maybe they had been wrong. Or maybe this was due to all the illnesses Maddie had as a baby, as a toddler, and as a preschooler, a result of being exposed to who knows what in daycare because I had chosen to work so much instead of being home with her more. Maybe I had made the wrong choice. I was tormented.

I remember walking down the hallway at work the day after we learned what was going on. I was 106 pounds, far too thin for my frame. I felt scared and weak, like I could be blown over by a gust of wind. Again, I was holding all this responsibility for my daughter's diagnosis. The one question running through my mind was, *How am I going to be able to live with myself?* The sheer terror from this question led me to eventually ask some other big questions: *What am I really responsible for? What is in my control versus not in my control in life?* Eventually, I asked, *If life is going to go on like this, if this is it, how am I going to choose to spend my days?*

The answer was, *I need to be doing meaningful work.*

If someone would have told me that, like Jess when she gained those eighty pounds, I was being given a gift with Maddie's diagnosis, I would have been downright angry, thinking that person was certainly not a parent of a child with special needs themselves.

Only now, many years later, I know this to be true; in fact, Maddie's diagnosis brought with it many more gifts than I could have imagined. They include:

- Knocking my priorities squarely into place. What really matters in life anyway?
- Learning to accept my child for who she is and who she is not.
- Learning to be okay with imperfection which, for a recovering perfectionist, isn't easy.
- Learning to powerfully stand for my child in the face of adversity.
- Creating a new relationship with patience—patience for my child and patience for people who don't understand her diagnosis.
- Connecting with parents of children with any special need or difference on a profound level.
- Breaking the destructive cycle of controlling and managing my family and other people in my life when I believed I always knew better.
- Being responsible to figure out my greater "what for," my purpose in life. Turns out it's pretty simple: to be of service to others.
- Maddie's diagnosis got me into action to follow my dreams.

In every challenge, we have choices. We can relate to it as a struggle, something we are affected by or have fallen victim to. We can sweep the "feels" and fears under the rug, pretending they don't exist.

Or, we can choose a path of responsibility. One where we face our deepest fears and angst head on in service of our children, our families, and ourselves. From this place, we are able to move through our challenges and heartbreak more powerfully, to become aware of the gifts available to us right now—today—in the present moment.[21]

Who will you be in the face of your life's challenges?

WELL-BEING EXERCISES

1. A regular Well-Being Tracking practice will help you notice where you are and are not taking actions to support your well-being. Make a list of five to seven habits that would support you if you did them on a daily basis. Use a simple chart with the habits down the side and the days of the week across the top. Then, track those habits daily. My mom was a speech therapist who worked from our home, and I remember the behavior modification charts she used with her students. Your well-being chart will be somewhat like that, but in addition to tracking progress, it will also uncover your predictable patterns. Examples of habits you can track:
   a. flossing your teeth
   b. stretching your body
   c. reading an inspirational article
   d. meditating
   e. calling a friend
   f. spending thirty minutes in nature
2. Gratitude practice: Write down three things you're grateful for three times a day (at each meal, for example). These things can be as big or small as you like. I remind my clients that having running water counts. And electricity!
3. Notice what's right or positive in a situation. Bringing in a different perspective is a powerful exercise for improving well-being.

GOLDEN KEYS

- What is ONE thing you'll take on today to honor your well-being? Warning: that critical voice in your head is going to tell you you're not the priority, you'll get to it later, you'll start tomorrow. As a leader, you are a model. You are a trainer. Your team and others who look to you for guidance are watching. Honor *you*.
- The power of simply being consistent is huge. Show up for yourself and others because you said you would. We've all started something with great intentions and commitment only to find ourselves stopping a few days, weeks, or months later. How do you stay on track with consistent action even when you don't want to?
- Who will you be when things don't unfurl as expected?

EQ CONNECTION: HAPPINESS

Happiness is your overall ability to enjoy life, to see things positively. Here is an example: I had a client, we'll call her Noelle, who came to me and was just exhausted. Noelle engaged me for a career move but everything we talked about had a sense of heaviness and obligation around it—even her kids. Her responsibilities with the kids felt like too much. She had to be up late, doing laundry for them, and then she'd wake up early in the morning so she could get her exercise in and get to work at a reasonable hour.

Noelle was clearly not happy, and had a general feeling of discontent with everything. On the weekends, she felt like she had to cram everything in to get stuff accomplished; otherwise, she was wasting time. It showed up in her relationship with her husband and it was showing up at work, which is why she had chosen to hire me.

After our first session, I was like, "Wow. No wonder you're exhausted."

The narrative in Noelle's brain, and all the negativity, was exhausting for me just hearing about it. And I don't mean that in a judgmental way. I was heartbroken for her as I was listening and thinking, *This is really heavy.*

So, we worked on shifting her thinking. We worked to change it—not to rose-colored glasses, but to a framework in which she could be grateful for all the little moments in her life that were positive or nice. This particular client had experienced a few deaths, people not super-close to her but close enough that she had gone to several funerals as we were working together. Every time there was a funeral, or she went to church and there was a particular prayer, it would wake her up to this new way of living and thinking.

Noelle was ready to heal things, to see things differently.

So, whenever there was this sense of *have to,* we worked on shifting it to *I get to; I have a choice.*

It wasn't *I should,* it was *I could.* And just these small shifts gave her more lightness and more freedom. Like many of my clients, she'd come to me for work on making new career pivot. She actually did make the pivot, but not till much later, after we stopped working together. But Noelle said that what she got from our time together was far more valuable than she could have ever imagined. And fortunately, we did set her up to be able to make the leap professionally. Even before that, she was able to really sink in and enjoy what she had and be grateful for it.

There's another client of mine, Wendy, who tended to have a similar narrative. The interesting thing about Wendy is we were talking last night about how she has been. She's had a major shift in her overall happiness since we've all been staying in our homes due to the COVID-19 pandemic. The reason is, she's working from home, so she doesn't have the long commute she used to. Wendy is no longer stressed about fitting everything in. She's able to enjoy the home she's built and has poured so much love into. She loves the freedom she's able to achieve in her life right now because she's not bound to a desk at work. She can do things for herself and now has more time for things like preparing well-balanced meals.

Even in the midst of a global health crisis, new opportunities for happiness are presenting themselves to people.

Overall happiness is really foundational to our well-being. And I don't mean just in terms of whether we are exercising, eating healthy, or drinking enough water. I am referring to the well-being of our thoughts—having compassion and kindness for ourselves. Giving ourselves breaks when we need to have them.

A New Beginning

SILENCE IS GOLDEN

Be more of who you truly are.

*P*eople spend their whole lives trying to achieve results. Yet I'll be the first to tell you that when they *get* the results, they're often frustrated because they don't feel any different. I was scared that when I became a coach—when I blew up my career and walked away from all I had created professionally—I would bump up against the same fears and bad feelings, but just be doing something I liked a little bit better. I remember a moment when I said to my sister, "What if I make this huge change and nothing feels different? What if I can never be satisfied?"

But that didn't happen.

Because when I walked away from my job and built my business, the circumstances of my life were not the only thing that changed. Much more significantly, *I* changed. When you do the work I've outlined in this book, you're changing the thought patterns in your gray matter. You're shifting your beliefs and expanding your possibilities.

I've always been drawn to results, so I get why I chose a career in coaching instead of in psychotherapy: to help clients create *results*. Today, however, I know my life's work is enabling me to surrender the importance I have previously placed on results—not to be so controlled or influenced by them. They don't always need to be perfect. No matter what happens on paper or in my bank account, I am still me. I still have down days. I still struggle. Having an orientation toward generating results is simply one more way to get a high, a good feeling. All this said, I don't want to completely negate the results I create for myself, for my family, and for my clients. Results are, in many ways, my brand. I'm your Type A coach.

But I want to leave you with more than results. I want to leave you with peace, and with the knowledge that no matter what's going on "out there," you are okay.

We are all okay.

My story goes back a long way because throughout my life, I've learned differently than others. I think differently. In fifth grade, the adults in my life thought I would continue to struggle given my learning differences. But then I ended up on the A track. In college, then in the corporate world, the same pattern repeated: I struggled during the first semester, wasn't sure I would make it through freshman year, and then I became really successful. It's all because of one word: commitment.

When I show up, I am all in. I'm committed to being successful, but in many different ways. Financially, sure, and deep down, I'm a profoundly spiritual person. And I have so much capacity for work, for family, and to be active in the community. I am gifted at what I do. I seek to making a difference for my clients—supporting them how they want to be supported.

I've had a lot of accomplishments, but more importantly, I am a life-long learner. I'm always looking for ways to improve. But there is a dark side to me as well. Sometimes, I can be too controlling. I can be vain: I like to be recognized for the contribution I'm making or for the generosity I have. The drawback of all my capacity is this: I know what it feels like to burn out, by saying *yes* when I really mean *no*. Or saying no, and then beating myself up for it. I'm constantly driven by a voice in my head that says, *What's next?* By a sense of *never enough*. A sense of *there's always more*, which can be overwhelming.

"Silence is Golden" refers to the new relationship I have learned to create with myself through activities like yoga, meditation, and being in nature. This mantra refers to the clarity that comes from quieting down and listening. Silence can be uncomfortable, for sure. But learning from that discomfort is a gift. My clients get to experience this kind of discomfort in our work together both in and outside of our sessions.

If you are committed to being successful, in ways you don't even yet know, and if you've been extraordinarily successful, even though deep down you sometimes feel like an imposter, then you and I should have a conversation.

What's Your Purpose?

If "purpose" is the reason why something exists, your life purpose is the reason *you* exist. Brooke Castillo teaches that we don't know our purpose, but that we'd better figure it out or it all will be wasted.[22] Every day for the last month, I journaled on what my purpose is. On day one, I wrote, "I am living my purpose, but sometimes I feel like I'm disappointing those around me who don't get it, who don't love their work."

Here is what came up for me over the course of the month: My purpose is to be an example of loving the work that you do and doing the work that you love. Not many people do. I almost feel a bit of shame; I love what I do so much and I'm so intense about it. I invite you to do this exercise as well; it's very powerful.

What do *I* want my purpose to be, versus what purpose is being given to me? It's really an intentional question. I want to be a model of what is possible in a career. I want people to know they can work a lot, love what they do, and not have to feel shame about it—especially women. I'm a model of strength as a woman; I demand for equality; I'm a model for not accepting abuse—verbal or otherwise—from a partner. I'm a model of someone who is unstoppable, an abundance-mindset model, a model of how your thoughts create your reality. I'm a model of not stopping at fear; of freedom that comes from being honest, authentic, and vulnerable with yourself and others; of understanding emotions in your career; and of unearthing your Golden Self as it relates to your professional self.

My purpose is to bring humor to heaviness. My purpose is aligned to my constant struggle with my weight, to be a model of love and acceptance, to have a career I love, to accept all of myself and all of life, and to live it authentically. I want to be exposed, vulnerable, fully-open, and living intentionally—not to be a victim of circumstances in any area, especially in my career. I strive to be highly self-aware and to set my life up accordingly, to be strong emotionally and physically, to learn when to be in the present and when to be future-focused.

My purpose is to be a message of what's possible, to inspire others to keep going and not give up on their dreams, to help people see what is blocking them, to remember what they imagined for themselves when they were children. I want to reflect the struggle and suffering we all experience when we live on autopilot; to share that there is another way, and that way is by managing our minds; and to remind people they are not alone. My purpose is to own my intensity and be proud of all I have accomplished.

It is important to me to be a role model as a mother, to normalize the experience of being an emotionally sensitive person, to raise strong children, to work on relationships and have them be lasting, to know my own power. To my clients and readers, I want to show it is possible to have everything you want with ease, to blow people away with my belief in myself while being coachable, honest, and vulnerable. My goal is to be a model of authenticity and vulnerability for Type A (plus!) women and men, and to recover from the grip of my perfectionism. My goal is to help people live a rich life, where they leave a legacy and make a difference.

What is your purpose? I invite you to start finding out.

Live

I was at the funeral of a dear friend's father recently. While sitting there in the pews, I noticed that very few people talked about what this man had done for a living. But they all talked about the essence of his soul and his being. For him, it had been positivity, love, and family.

I often ask my clients, "Will this matter at the end of your life?" referring to whatever it is they're concerned about. So, when you are setting *your* big vision, who is it you want to be?

There was no question about the fact that this man, this father of my friend, had been exactly who he had chosen to be. In his eighty years, he had lived life to the fullest. Two of his four grandkids and all three of his kids spoke that day, giving intricate details about who he was ... the way he ordered his food at restaurants, the types of jokes he made.

There were all of these stories dating back to my friend's childhood in the 1970s. There was so much laughter and giggling, even in the midst of the loss. It was obvious my friend's father was a man who had given so much to each individual person in his life.

He loved each person uniquely, and made each of them feel so special. He was unwilling to compromise on the things that were most important to him—his family, his religion, his traditions, and being a good person.

At the end of your life, do you want to look back and say, I *lived*?

This man definitely had.

Will you?

About the Author

EMILY **GOLDEN** helps today's emerging leaders and executives shift underlying beliefs, find their sweet spot, and bring new-found value to their careers.

Recognized as an expert in Emotional Intelligence in the workplace, Emily incorporates her years of corporate human resources experience into her high-performance coaching practice. She is familiar with the challenges executives face, including time management, overwork, and the potential for burnout. Her clients emerge re-energized, equipped with the tools that help them create a balanced and meaningful life *inside and outside of work*.

No stranger to the delicate balance of work-life juggling, Emily was a top performer when a troubling diagnosis struck her family. Her daughter was diagnosed with Tourette Syndrome in 2010. Despite the emotional toll, Emily's perfectionism kicked in and she was determined to be the best wife, mother, and employee.

The trouble was, at home, she was thinking about work. At work, she was thinking about what she needed to do for her kids at home. When her son was also diagnosed with the same syndrome in 2013, Emily shifted her focus to finding a workable balance that honored her capacity in both her work and her personal life.

She realized that her talents for seeing both the blind spots and the skills in others in her corporate position translated seamlessly into coaching those high performers looking to advance professionally, while avoiding the traps of burnout, or of "golden handcuffs," those financial benefits provided by an employer to discourage an employee from leaving.

Combining her leadership and work in human resources for over seventeen years, Emily has created a powerful coaching method not typically offered in corporate America. As a professional, certified coach with over 2,500 coaching hours, Emily combines assessment tools, including EQi 2.0™, with her step-by-step transformational approach that she has honed and developed through her work with hundreds of clients.

"As a professional coach, I'm particularly passionate about supporting my clients—from executives to emerging leaders—as they climb the professional ladder without sacrificing their fulfilling personal lives. And I promise you, it doesn't have to be exhausting to actually achieve this. Because there isn't one right way to integrate financial or job security with your personal and family life. There's simply your way."

thenewgoldenrule.info

Endnotes

1   National Historic Park Service, National Historical Park, New Jersey, "Thomas Edison," Accessed March 10, 2020, https://www.nps.gov/edis/learn/education/index.htm

2   Neff, Kristin, *Self-Compassion: The Proven Power of Being Kind to Yourself* (New York: William Morrow, 2011).

3   Oprah Winfrey Network, "Why Brené Brown Says Perfectionism Is a 20-Ton Shield," YouTube, October 6, 2013, https://www.youtube.com/watch?v=o7yYFHyvweE&feature=youtube.

4   Forleo, Marie, *Everything Is Figureoutable* (New York: Portfolio Books, 2019).

5   Stein, Steven J, and Howard E. Book, *The EQ Edge* (San Francisco: Jossey-Bass, 2011).

6   Dyer, Dr. Wayne W., "Success Secrets," *Wayne's Blog* (blog), *Dr. Wayne W. Dyer,* October, 2009, https://www.drwaynedyer.com/blog/success-secrets/

7   Hay, Louise L., *You Can Heal Your Life* (Carlsbad: Hay House, Inc. 1984).

8   Hendricks, Gay, *The Big Leap* (New York: HarperOne, 2019).

9   Stein, Steven J, and Howard E. Book, *The EQ Edge.*

10 Brown, Brené, *Dare to Lead: Brave Work. Tough Conversations. Whole Hearts.* (New York: Random House, 2018).

11 Harris, Russ, *The Confidence Gap: A Guide to Overcoming Fear and Self-Doubt* (Boston: Trumpeter Books, 2011).

12 Next Step Partners, "Vision," in *Imagine, Plan, Succeed: Career Handbook for Working Professionals,* 2nd ed. (Stanford: New Step Partners, 2014) 34–35.

13 Next Step Partners, "Vision," 34–35.

14 Next Step Partners, "Vision," 34–35.

15 Forleo, Marie, Everything Is Figureoutable (New York: Portfolio Books, 2019).

16 The Live Coach School, "Self Coaching Model," June 6, 2019, https://thelifecoachschool.com/self-coaching-model/.

17 Stein, Steven J, and Howard E. Book, *The EQ Edge.*

18 Goodreads, Quotable Quote: "Helen Keller," Accessed July 30, 2020. https://www.goodreads.com/quotes/818488-although-the-world-is-full-of-suffering-it-is-full

19 Golden, Emily, "Worry Free Living Month," *TS Parents Online,* December 1, 2016, https://njcts.org/tsparents/2016/12/01/worry-free-living-month/

20 Beck, Martha, "How to Tap Into Your True Power," *O, The Oprah Magazine,* September, 2009, https://www.oprah.com/spirit/how-to-battle-powerlessness-martha-beck/

21 Golden, Emily, "Who Will You Be in the Face of Your Child's Differences," *TS Parents Online,* November 16, 2016, https://njcts.org/tsparents/2016/11/16/who-will-you-be-in-the-face-of-your-childs-differences/

22 Castillo, Brooke, "Knowing versus Not Knowing," The Life Coach School, Accessed March 10, 2020, https://thelifecoachschool.com/podcast/106/

Bibliography

Beck, Martha. "How to Tap Into Your True Power." *O, The Oprah Magazine*. September, 2009. https://www.oprah.com/spirit/how-to-battle-powerlessness-martha-beck/

Brown, Brené. *Dare to Lead: Brave Work. Tough Conversations. Whole Hearts*. New York: Random House, 2018.

Castillo, Brooke. "Knowing versus Not Knowing." The Life Coach School. Accessed March 10, 2020. https://thelifecoachschool.com/podcast/106/

Dyer, Dr. Wayne W. "Success Secrets." *Wayne's Blog* (blog). *Dr. Wayne W. Dyer*, October, 2009. https://www.drwaynedyer.com/blog/success-secrets/

Forleo, Marie. *Everything Is Figureoutable*. New York: Portfolio Books, 2019.

Goodreads. "Helen Keller." Quotes, Quotable Quote. Accessed March 10, 2020. https://www.goodreads.com/quotes/818488-although-the-world-is-full-of-suffering-it-is-full

Golden, Emily. "Who Will You Be in the Face of Your Child's Differences?" *TS Parents Online*. November 16, 2016. https://njcts.org/tsparents/2016/11/16/who-will-you-be-in-the-face-of-your-childs-differences/

Golden, Emily. "Worry Free Living Month." *TS Parents Online.* December 1, 2016. https://njcts.org/tsparents/2016/12/01/worry-free-living-month/

Harris, Russ. *The Confidence Gap: A Guide to Overcoming Fear and Self-Doubt.* Boston: Trumpeter Books, 2011.

Hay, Louise L. *You Can Heal Your Life.* Carlsbad: Hay House, Inc. 1984.

Hendricks, Gay. *The Big Leap.* New York: HarperOne, 2019.

Keller, Helen. *The Story of My Life.* New York: Bantam, 1902.

National Historic Park Service, National Historical Park, New Jersey. "Thomas Edison." Accessed March 10, 2020. https://www.nps.gov/edis/learn/education/index.htm

Neff, Kristin. *Self-Compassion: The Proven Power of Being Kind to Yourself.* New York: William Morrow, 2011.

The Life Coach School. "Self Coaching Model." June 6, 2019. https://thelifecoachschool.com/self-coaching-model/

Stein, Steven J, and Howard E. Book. *The EQ Edge.* San Francisco: Jossey-Bass, 2011.

CPSIA information can be obtained
at www.ICGtesting.com
Printed in the USA
BVHW031815190920
589120BV00001B/43